# Keto Diet Instant Pot Cookbook

*The Complete Ketogenic Instant Pot Cookbook - Quick, Easy and Delicious Ketogenic Recipes made for Your Instant Pot*

# Table of Contents

Introduction ........................................................................................................ 7

The Ketogenic Diet ............................................................................................ 8

  Is the ketogenic diet for everyone? ............................................................. 9

  What do you eat on a ketogenic diet? ......................................................... 9

  Foods to Avoid on the Keto Diet ............................................................... 10

  Foods to Eat on the Keto Diet ................................................................... 11

  Benefits of the Ketogenic Diet ................................................................... 11

The Instant Pot ................................................................................................ 14

  What is the Instant Pot ............................................................................... 14

  Using the Buttons on the Instant Pot ........................................................ 16

Benefits of Using the Instant Pot .................................................................... 21

Ketogenic Instant Pot Recipes ........................................................................ 27

  Instant Pot Ketogenic Breakfast Recipes .................................................. 27

    Keto Egg Cups on the Go ......................................................................... 27

    Boiled Eggs in the Instant Pot .................................................................. 28

    Coconut Milk Yogurt ................................................................................ 29

    Sous Vide Bacon Egg Bites "Starbucks" Style ....................................... 30

    Keto Poblano Cheese Frittata ................................................................... 32

    Spinach, Tomato and Feta Egg Cups ....................................................... 33

    Mini-Mushroom Quiche ........................................................................... 34

  Instant Pot Ketogenic Soup and Stew Recipes .......................................... 35

    Jalapeno Popper Soup ............................................................................... 35

    Unstuffed Cabbage Soup .......................................................................... 37

    Low Carb Taco Soup ................................................................................ 38

    Jalapeno Cheeseburger Spicy Soup .......................................................... 39

Cabbage-Beef Soup...........................................................................41

Creamy Chicken-Bacon Chowder .................................................42

Loaded Cauliflower Soup ...............................................................43

Buffalo Chicken Soup ....................................................................45

Italian Sausage Kale Soup.............................................................46

Egg Roll Soup ................................................................................47

Easy Broccoli Cheddar Soup .........................................................48

Zuppa Toscana Soup .....................................................................49

## Instant Pot Ketogenic Meat Recipes .........................................50

Balsamic Pot Roast........................................................................50

Smothered Pork Chops ..................................................................51

Italian Meatballs............................................................................53

Chicken Crack!...............................................................................54

Jamaican Jerk Roast .....................................................................55

Italian Braised Chicken .................................................................56

Bolognese for the Instant Pot........................................................57

Barbacoa (Chipotle Copy) .............................................................58

Orange Turkey ...............................................................................60

Low Carb Pork Ribs.......................................................................62

Chicken Cacciatore ........................................................................63

Garlic Chipotle Lime Chicken .......................................................64

Pot Roast with Chimichurri Sauce................................................65

Lamb Barbacoa..............................................................................67

Chicken Tikka Masala ...................................................................68

Hot Wings......................................................................................69

## Instant Pot Ketogenic Seafood Recipes.....................................71

Lemon & Peppered Salmon ...........................................................71

Alaskan Cod...................................................................................72

Salmon with Chili-Lime Sauce......................................................73

Brazilian Fish Stew .......................................................................74

Keto Shrimp Scampi......................................................................75

Asian Salmon and Vegetables .......................................................76

Indian Shrimp Curry....................................................................78

Seafood Gumbo..........................................................................79

Fish Chowder ............................................................................81

Instant Pot Ketogenic Vegan Recipes........................................82

Butternut Squash Soup..............................................................82

Cauliflower Mushroom Soup.....................................................83

Brussels Sprouts Side................................................................84

Cabbage Soup............................................................................85

Flavored Cauli-Rice...................................................................86

Sri Lankan Coconut Cabbage ...................................................88

Pressure Steamed Artichoke......................................................89

Creamy Cauliflower Soup .........................................................90

Vegan Cream of Asparagus Soup...............................................91

Instant Pot Ketogenic Vegetarian Recipes ................................92

Soy Curl Butter "Chicken" ........................................................92

Mashed Cauliflower ..................................................................93

Zucchini and Yellow Squash Soup.............................................94

Garlic Ginger Red Cabbage.......................................................95

Vegetarian Cream of Asparagus Soup........................................96

Cream of Celery Soup................................................................97

Instant Pot Ketogenic Main Course Recipes .............................98

Corned Beef and Cabbage Dinner .............................................98

Indian Kheema..........................................................................99

Italian Pulled Pork Ragu.........................................................100

Ground Beef Shawarma...........................................................101

Creamy Salsa Chicken.............................................................102

Green Chili Pork Taco Bowl....................................................104

No Noodle Lasagna..................................................................105

Creamy Chicken and Broccoli Casserole .................................106

Sausage, Zucchini and Cauliflower Risotto..............................107

Stuffed Pepper Casserole ........................................................108

Pork Chops with Cabbage........................................................109

Pork and Kraut ....................................................................................................110

Hungarian Goulash ............................................................................................... 111

Pulled Pork Carnitas.............................................................................................113

Boeuf Bourguignon with Veggies ........................................................................115

## Instant Pot Ketogenic Side Dish Recipes ....................................................117

Cauliflower Rice and Cheese ............................................................................... 117

Spaghetti Squash with Sage-Garlic Sauce ..........................................................118

Zoodles with Lemon, Garlic and Parmesan.........................................................119

Bacon Parmesan Spaghetti Squash ..................................................................... 120

Brussels Sprouts with Bacon................................................................................121

Asparagus Wrapped in Prosciutto ....................................................................... 122

Ham and Greens.................................................................................................... 123

Carrot Pasta .......................................................................................................... 124

Spinach and Artichoke Dip (Like Applebee's!) ................................................. 125

Creamed Cauliflower and Spinach....................................................................... 126

## Conclusion ............................................................................................................127

# Introduction

Many people have been successful in achieving health benefits and losing weight by following a ketogenic diet. The eating plan has been gaining in popularity, and for good reason. Most find that it works, and works well. Following the diet is not difficult and the included foods are typically items on hand.

The keto diet is a high fat, low carb diet. By eating certain foods and avoiding others the body's metabolism and energy consumption is switched. It is known by a few other names such as ketogenic diet, ketosis diet, low carb high fat (LCHF) diet or just a low carb diet. There are a few ways in which a low carb diet and the ketogenic diet are comparable. The term, "low carb" can mean different things to different people. In general, restricting the amount of carbohydrates you consume is low carb. However, with a typical low carb diet, the brain is not going to make the switch from depending on glucose as fuel source. We'll explain more about how this process works. But low carb diets alone can vary greatly in the amount of carbohydrates you can consume each day. There are many different opinions and guidelines for how many carbs should be eaten. It literally ranges from zero to a hundred.

Thanks to the innovation of the Instant Pot cooking prep and time can be reduced significantly. Here you'll find more about the ketogenic diet, and how it can benefit you, as well as how you can do a significant amount of cooking in the Instant Pot saving you a lot of time.

# The Ketogenic Diet

The ketogenic diet is a specific way of eating that helps the body achieve a state of ketosis. The dieting plan focuses on consuming fewer carbohydrates, moderate protein and more (good) fats. The body makes ketones, which are small fuel molecules. These are created in the body and are used as fuel to energize the body, if there is not an adequate supply of glucose.

Carbohydrates are broken down very quickly in the body and become blood sugar. When you reduce the amount of carbs eaten, the body switches to producing ketones. The liver produces ketones from the fat that is eaten. The brain uses a lot of energy. It uses about 25% of the body's energy. Because of its need for energy, it's hungry for something to use for it. But the brain doesn't run directly on fat. It only runs on glucose, or ketones.

When you begin eating a ketogenic diet, the body will automatically switch to fat for fuel. This will help insulin levels drop and increase the amount of fat the body burns. This process makes it easier for the body to burn off stored fat supplies. There are several benefits that will be discussed a little later, but the obvious benefit is that you will lose weight as the body burns off stored fat.

*Ketosis vs. Glycolysis*

When the body is using glucose, or sugar, for it's primary energy source, it is in the state of glycolysis. Ketosis is achieved when metabolic state of the body switches over to using ketone bodies in the blood for it's main energy source. Individuals who do not control their intake of carbohydrates, stay in the state of glycolysis. However, there are a few reasons why it's beneficial to be in a state of ketosis rather than glycolysis.

*Keto and Insulin*

When the body reaches the desired state of ketosis, it runs on ketones. Ketones are produced in the liver once the glycogen has been depleted. Ketones burn slower as a fuel source. By eating a diet high in carbohydrates, your body continuously creating insulin in order to transport glucose throughout the body. This lets fat just sit around since the insulin is basically doing all the work. Once the fat sits for a while, it is eventually stored. The result is unwanted weight gain. Once the body reaches ketosis, the body starts breaking down the fat in the liver and converts it into ketones. And they are of course, used for energy. This helps maintain a stable level of insulin and inhibits the body from storing fat. The process helps you maintain your weight and encourages weight loss.

## Is the ketogenic diet for everyone?

In general, the ketogenic diet is safe. There are a few instances when a person may need to seek the advice of a medical professional before starting. These situations may require assistance:

- If you are taking medication for diabetes. (Insulin)
- If you are taking blood pressure medication.
- If you are breastfeeding.

If you are on medications prescribed by a doctor, it's just smart to discuss starting any diet plan with them before beginning.

## What do you eat on a ketogenic diet?

Achieving ketosis means eating macronutrients in certain ratios. Remember, you want more fats, focusing on good fats, moderate protein and low amounts of carbohydrates. The basic break down of macronutrient consumption looks something like this:

- 60 to 80 percent of your total calories should come from fat.
- 15 to 35 percent of total calories should come from protein.

- 5 percent or less of your caloric intake should come from carbohydrates.

Of course, each person is different, and this can vary a bit between individuals. When you follow this ratio for macronutrients, your body will be depleted of its glucose and forced into producing ketones. Once the body makes ketones, it will start using them for an energy source instead. So, what should you eat and what should you avoid?

## Foods to Avoid on the Keto Diet

There are certain foods you need to avoid. Avoid sugars of all kinds as well as starchy foods. Potatoes, bread, pasta, and rice are all starchy. When starch is consumed it becomes glucose or sugar. You will want to restrict your intake of carbs but keep it high in fat, with a limited amount of protein. As a rough guideline, you want your carb intake to be between 5 and 10% the lower the better. Specifically, you will want to avoid foods such as:

- Foods with Sugar: Sodas, smoothies, ice cream, fruit juice, candy, etc.
- Starches Including Grains: Pasta, cereal, rice, bread, wheat-based products
- Fruit: avoid most fruits (some berries are allowed)
- Legumes/beans: chickpeas, lentils, peas, kidney beans, pintos, etc.
- Tubers and root vegetables: all potatoes, parsnips, carrots, etc.
- Diet foods: Low-fat other foods labeled as "diet foods" are highly processed. Most of them are high in carbohydrates. Sugar-free foods are taboo as well since they typically are high in sugar alcohols. These can affect ketone levels. They are also typically highly processed.
- Unhealthy fats: Restrict intake of processed oils like vegetable oils and mayonnaise.
- Sauces/condiments: Check labels as some are okay but may contain unhealthy fats and sugars.
- Alcohol: Alcoholic beverages are generally high in carbs and should be avoided.

## Foods to Eat on the Keto Diet

Remember eating the proper ratio of fat, protein and carbs is what helps you achieve ketosis. To be successful, stick with foods such as:

- Meats: chicken, turkey, sausage, ham, steak and other red meats
- Fatty fish: tuna, mackerel, trout and salmon for example
- Eggs: eat whole pastured or omega-3 eggs
- Cheese: unprocessed cheeses like cheddar, cream, mozzarella, blue and goat cheese
- Healthy oils: coconut oil, avocado oil and extra virgin olive oil are best
- Butter/cream: eat grass-fed options when possible
- Nuts/Seeds: chia seeds, pumpkin seeds, flaxseeds, walnuts and almonds
- Avocados: fresh avocados
- Veggies (Low carb): green vegetables, tomatoes, peppers, onions, etc.
- Condiments: salt, pepper, herbs and spices (read the label to avoid sugar and processed foods and fats)

## Benefits of the Ketogenic Diet

For many years, people were afraid of low-carb diets, and for a while they were mostly controversial. Add to that the fact that the media and health professionals were promoting fat-phobic messages and a lot of people refrained from ketogenic and other low carbohydrate diets. They wrongly assumed these types of diets could lead to heart disease because of the fat intake which was thought to contribute to raised cholesterol.

However, over the last 15 years or so, there have been several studies directed at low-carb diets. In almost every single study, the low carbohydrate diet far surpassed the ones they were being comparted to. Finally, it is commonly believed a low carb diet helps with weight loss efforts as well as improving many risk factors, including cholesterol. While individual results can vary because each person is unique, there are several health benefits that many can achieve by following the ketogenic diet.

*Decreases the Appetite* – When your diet contains more fat, you are likely to feel fuller longer. One reason people give up on a diet is because they are hungry and miserable. A ketogenic diet includes less carbs, but more fat which burns off more slowly. The lower intake of carbs can lead to a reduction in the amount of foods you desire.

*Weight Loss* – For most people, cutting carbs equates to weight loss. When fewer carbs are consumed, most individuals tend to lose more weight than those who observe a low-fat diet. The weight loss, is typically faster as well.

*Increased "Good" Cholesterol* – High-density lipoprotein, or HDL, is referred to as the good kind of cholesterol. Both LDL and HDL are lipoproteins that carry the cholesterol around the body through the blood. LDL is responsible for carrying cholesterol out of the liver to the rest of the body. HDL carries cholesterol from the body, to the liver. The liver then excretes it, or reuses it. The keto diet helps increase HDL levels while raising HDL levels. Improvements in this ratio are said to help lower the risk of developing heart disease.

*Increased Energy* – Almost everyone who switches to the keto diet notices increased, and better sustained, energy levels. When energy levels are stabilized, it's likely for a person to avoid the mid-afternoon slump. There is also fewer (or no) sugar or caffeine cravings. Why? Mostly because fat becomes a readily available fuel source. Once they are into ketosis, most people find they can go longer periods of time without drastic swings in their energy levels.

*Reduces Risk of Some Types of Cancer* – Some studies are currently being done to determine if a ketogenic diet can help prevent, or treat some cancers. Some theories exist suggesting that since the ketogenic diet reduces high blood sugar for some people, it may also be able to reduce insulin complications which may also be associated with a few types of cancer. Presently, the ketogenic diet is thought to be beneficial for patients undergoing chemotherapy or radiation treatments for cancer.

*Lower Inflammation and Reduce Pain* – Ketosis is beneficial for some individuals who suffer from pain and inflammation. Reducing the metabolism of glucose can have an influence on pain. There are several studies being conducted now to determine what extent ketosis may be able to help reduce pain and inflammation.

*Fights Aging* – If you can lower the oxidative stress in your body, you may be able to increase your lifespan. Ketosis works to lower insulin levels, which also reduces the body's oxidative stress. There are some experts who feel a ketogenic diet slows down the effects of aging.

*Reduces the Effects of Several Health Conditions* – Once the body goes into ketosis, it is highly likely you are going to feel better in general. There are still lots of studies and research projects being conducted at this time, but eating a keto lifestyle may be able to help prevent or reduce the effects of these conditions:

- Metabolic Syndrome
- Polycystic Ovary Syndrome
- Irritable Bowel Syndrome
- Fatty Liver Disease
- Migraine Headaches
- Mood Instability
- Parkinson's and Alzheimer's Disease
- Epilepsy
- Acne

Each person's metabolic makeup differs, but most people benefit greatly once they switch to the keto diet. For some, the benefit is immediate and easily discerned. For others, it takes some time to feel the actual result.

# The Instant Pot

## What is the Instant Pot

The Instant Pot is one of the hottest crazes that has hit cooking in a long time. In all likelihood you've seen recipes, blogs and plenty of online buzz about it. Maybe you've even been wondering what all the talk is about. Describing the Instant Pot is somewhat difficult since it is useful for so many things. It is a multi-functional cooker. Just one pot can perform the job of several appliances. There are several different models available and some have more features than others. However, it is multifunctional and can perform a variety of tasks.

Depending on the model purchased, it can be used as a slow cooker, pressure cooker, rice cooker, Dutch oven, and that's just the beginning. Sautee' or steam veggies, or brown meat. Some models also have a yogurt making feature. If you are looking for the perfect all-in-one cooker, this is it.

*Using the Instant Pot for a Slow Cooker*
Slow cookers or crock pots have been popular for years because you can toss in a few ingredients, walk away and come home to supper. The instant pot is just a little more than a crock pot. For instance, it is designed with a microprocessor that can adjust heat levels, so you'll get consistent results. Another feature that enhances the slow cooker is the 24-hour timer. It can be used to make sure food is kept warm until you're ready to serve it. These features make it a good option for large batches of food.

*Using it for a Pressure Cooker*
The pressure cooker feature of the instant pot is probably one of the best-known functions of this handy device. Many people have been afraid of using a pressure cooker in the past,

and some still are. It only takes one accident with the steam valve or blown off lid to earn your respect. This is why many people shy away from the traditional pressure cooking method. Thankfully, pressure cooking has evolved, and the Instant Pot can help remove the elements of guesswork and fear. It's about as easy as it gets. You select the setting and forget about it for a bit. You don't have to stand over the stove adjusting and readjusting the heat to make sure the pressure doesn't go too high or drop too low. This modern convenience lets you cook perfect creamy beans straight from the dried state without any presoaking. Or make hard-boiled eggs or baked potatoes in a matter of a few minutes. You can even cook an entire chicken in under an hour. The pot has built-in features to indicate when the lid is locked safely and wen it's safe to open it again.

*Cooking Grains in the Instant Pot*
If your instant pot has the grains or rice feature, you can make a bowl of rice or oatmeal quickly and easily.

*It's Just a Cooking Pot*
The Instant Pot is also good for lots of general cooking jobs. Sautee' peppers and onions, steam veggies, or use it for browning meat. It's generally best to brown meat before cooking it anyway. Using the Instant Pot helps reduce the number of pans you have to cleanup later.

*Use it for Baking*
You can bake a wide variety of desserts in the Instant Pot. For your next get together you can bake up a cheesecake, custard, pudding, fruit cobbler or bread pudding. Some like to use it to bake quick breads.

*Try it for Making Yogurt*
If your IP includes the feature, you can even use it to make yogurt.

# Using the Buttons on the Instant Pot

There can be any number of buttons and features included on your IP depending on which model is purchased. There are 7 basic buttons, or features to consider. If the unit has 7 functions, it will have 14 to 16 buttons if you include the + and − buttons when counting. Your pot will likely have at least 7 programmable functions.

- Pressure Cooking
- Slow Cooking
- Rice or Porridge Maker
- Steam Feature
- Sauté' or Browning Feature
- Yogurt Maker
- Warmer or Cancel Button

Here is a look at the buttons you may find on your instant pot if you already have one. If you are planning on purchasing one soon, most models will have these buttons or some combination of them. Make sure to get the model that includes the buttons you want.

*Pressure Cooker Button*

The pressure cooking button is also called the "manual" button because it allows you to set the time you want the pot to pressure cook the contents. Each recipe will tell you how long to pressure the contents, so you get the desired results. Press the +/- buttons to adjust the pressure and the length of time it cooks. It's important to note two things when using the pressure cooking feature. One, note how much liquid is to be added, usually one-half to one cup at least. Also note whether they are to be cooked on low or high setting and adjust accordingly. The manual, or pressure buttons are only used when pressure cooking they will not make adjustments for other functions such as the slow cooker, yogurt making or sautéing.

*Sautee Button*

You will probably use this feature more than you realize. It is very handy when cooking meats or dishes with veggies. This function saves you from having to use another skillet or pan. You just put a little oil in the bottom of the pot and add the food you want to sauté. Some Instant Pots have a temperature gauge. Normal mode is between 320 and 349 degrees F. Less mode is between 275 and 302 degrees F, and the More mode is from 347 to 410 degrees F. This feature is handy as you can brown veggies or meats then add other ingredients for your main dish and close the lid to pressure cook it in the same pot.

*Slow Cooker Setting*

This setting lets you make a crock pot out of your IP. Add the food to the inner pan just like you would to a slow cooker. Close the lid and then press "slow cook." The default cook time is 4 hours, but you can use the +/- buttons to adjust the cooking time.

*Bean and Chili Button*

Cooking beans in the crock pot has been a wonderful option, but you're going to love the pressure cooking abilities of the Instant Pot. Beans, or homemade chili can take hours in the slow cooker, and of course, you can still use the slow cooker setting if that works with your schedule. However, the 'bean/chili' button will cook beans faster. It has a default setting of 30 minutes, but it can be adjusted. Refer to your Instant Pot manual for cooking times for specific types of beans. Typically, kidney beans take about 20 to 25 minutes and black beans take 10 to 15 minutes.

*Stew and Meat Setting*

One of the best things about the stew and meat button is you can adjust it to achieve the texture you want. It defaults to high pressure and cooks for 35 minutes. Adjust it to more time if you want softer, fall-off-the-bone type meats. Or if you don't want mushy vegetables, adjust it to less time. Start with about 20 minutes to see if you get the desired results.

*Multigrain Setting*

The multigrain button is used to cook wild rice or brown rice. They usually take longer to cook than white rice. Use a ratio of 1 to 1.25 rice to water for brown rice. Wild rice needs a ratio of 1to3, rice to water. These should cook in between 22 and 30 minutes.

*Porridge Button*

The porridge button is used to make rice porridge, or congee. It will also make porridge with grains other than white or brown rice. The default setting is high pressure for 20 minutes, that works perfect for rice porridge. It can be adjusted to pressure for up to 30 minutes or down to 15 to get the texture you desire.

*Poultry Setting*

The Instant Pot is a wonderful option for making all your favorite chicken recipes. The "poultry" button defaults to high pressure for 15 minutes. However, it is easily adjusted to longer or shorter times depending on what you are cooking.

*Rice Setting*

The "rice" button on the Instant Pot is used for making white rice, Jasmine, Basmati or short grain rice. These can be cooked in less than 10 minutes, usually between 4 and 8 minutes. Usually, a ratio of 1to1 rice to water works well. However, Basmati requires a bit more water and a rice to water ratio of 1 to 1.5. When you are using the "rice" button, how long it cooks depends on how much food you put in the pot. You can also cook rice using the "manual" mode on high pressure.

*Soup Setting*

The soup setting is used for soup, of course, but it is also a great way to make broth or stock. The default settings control pressure levels so the liquid doesn't boil too heavily. Adjust the time for what you are making, but usually these need between 20 and 40 minutes.

*Steam Button*

The steam button is great for steaming seafood or vegetables. But it is also good for reheating food, especially if you are looking for an alternative for the microwave. Be sure to use the steam rack that came with your Instant Pot to prevent foods from burning or sticking. Add one to two cups of water in the pot then place the steam rack inside. Put the stainless-steel steam basket on top of the rack and add the food you want to steam. A filet of fresh fish, or frozen corn on the cob usually take three to five minutes, fresh foods like artichokes take up to nine to 11 minutes. Be sure to use the manual that came with your instant pot to determine the right amount of time to cook your foods.

*Yogurt Setting*

You can use your Instant Pot to make yogurt, but it's two steps. Put a cup of water in the inner pot and add milk to glass containers. Place the steam rack in the pot and place the glass containers with milk on top of it. Press the "steam" function and set it for a minute. Use natural release.

Then, leave the water in the pot and let the milk cool to below 115 degrees. After it has cooled, add yogurt starter or some yogurt from another batch. Push the "yogurt" button and select "normal" mode. Adjust the time depending on your recipe. When it is done, the display will read, "yogt."

*Egg Setting*

The latest instant pots come with an egg setting. Put eggs and water in the instant pot. Turn the steam valve to "sealed" and then press the "egg" button. It makes hard-boiled eggs. If you prefer soft-boiled eggs, use the "-" button to reduce cooking time to four minutes instead of five. Some pots include a special egg tray which can be used to make poached eggs. Follow the directions that came with your instant pot to make poached eggs.

*Cake Setting*

The cake setting can be used for breads or cakes. You will need cake and baking accessories to use this feature.

*Keep Warm and Cancel Buttons*

After the pot has completed use the "keep warm button to keep it warm until you are ready to serve it. "Cancel" will stop the pressure cooking mode. After the cooking is complete, the IP will beep. It will automatically go into "keep warm" mode. The display will have an "L" and a number to let you know how long it's been keeping warm. The "cancel" button is used to cancel cooking you have started. It can also be used to turn off the keep warm feature. This is nice for those times you chose the wrong time or for some other reason need to stop and adjust either the pressure or the time.

*Timer*

The timer button can be used to delay the start time for cooking in the IP. It works for both slow cooking and pressure cooking options. Once you place the food in the IP and set it for the desired cook method and time, you have 10 seconds to press the "timer" button. Use the up and down arrows to select how long you want to delay the start of cooking. Once you have it set for the desired delay time, press the "timer" again to set it. At any point, you can cancel the timer by pressing "cancel."

# Benefits of Using the Instant Pot

For each person who uses an Instant Pot for meal preparation, the specific benefits can vary. However, there are many advantages to using an Instant Pot. There are benefits you'll realize from using a pressure cooker specifically. Combine those benefits with the other features and you have a winning combination of lots of advantages. You can probably come up with a list of your own advantages, but let's look at a few of the prominent benefits most enjoy from using the IP.

### *Saving Time and Energy*

Pressure cooking is a much faster method for cooking foods safely. For the most part, an electric pressure cooker reduces cooking time by as much as 70% over other cooking methods. The pot itself, uses less energy since there isn't as much water used in the cooking process. With a fully insulated external pot, not as much water is necessary. Electric pressure cookers are ranked as second when it comes to energy efficient cooking appliances, that's just behind microwaves.

### *Preserves Nutrients*

Pressure cooking delivers an even, deep heat and distributes it quickly. This is the reason you do not have to fully immerse food in water, you just need enough to create some steam to build up the pressure. Sine the food is not submerged in water, the nutrients do not seep out of the food into the water. Steam surrounds food which means they do not become oxidized because of exposure air. If you notice, bright green veggies like broccoli retain those colors after cooking. The cooked food retains the original flavor. You may also notice while the IP is cooking, there is no smell of food wafting through the house. This is because the pot is sealed and holding in the nutrients.

### *Eliminate Dangerous Micro-Organisms*

Pressure cookers use temperatures above the boiling point. This is high enough to kill most of the harmful micro-organisms like viruses and bacteria. A pressure cooker can also be used to sterilize jam pots and glass baby bottles. They've also been used to treat water. Some of the latest Instant Pots have a "sterilize' button for this purpose.

Many foods like corn, beans and rice are carriers for aflatoxins, or fungal poisons. The occur naturally in foods, usually because of improper storage practices. Humid conditions can encourage the growth of fungi. Aflatoxins have been known to trigger liver cancer and may possibly contribute to other types of cancers too. Heating food to the boiling point does not kill aflatoxins. Recent studies have indicated that pressure cooking does reduce the concentration of aflatoxins to a safe level.

## Specific Instant Pot Benefits

Pressure cooking itself obviously has some advantages including health related ones. But there are also benefits that are more specific to using the Instant Pot itself, beyond just the pressure cooker feature. Here are a few of the benefits you will find as you venture into the world of the instant Pot.

### *Convenience*

Depending on the model you invest in, you'll find anywhere from 5 or 6 single-key operation buttons to 12. These include a variety of common cooking tasks. These are as simple as placing the food in the pot, sealing it and pushing a button. Here are a few of the buttons you'll find convenient:

- Rice (white and multigrain settings)
- Porridge
- Sautee' or browning
- Soup
- Meat and stew
- Beans/chili

- Poultry
- Steaming
- Slow cook (old fashioned crock pot feature)
- Keep warm
- Yogurt

All the single button operation keys were designed specifically to help you achieve consistent results with your cooking. There is also the option of using the manual pressure cooking button, so you can set the time your own recipes are cooked under pressure.

*Programming*

The on-button keys are pre-programed based on literally thousands of cooking experiments. They are pre-set to help you achieve the best result with your cooking ventures. Each button can also be refined to vary the taste from rare, normal or well done as per your family's preference.

*Automatic Cooking*

IP provides a lot of convenience by automating the cooking process. Each task is appropriately times and then automatically switches to the "keep warm" setting once cooking has completed. Conventional pressure cookers there isn't a timer, or food monitoring. You must manually keep the time and adjust the heat and length of time foods cook under pressure manually.

*Delayed Cooking Feature*

Just for a little more convenience, you can use the IP to delay cooking time up to 24 hours. This allows you to plan meals ahead of time. You are not required to stand over the stove and monitor your food's cooking. You don't even have to be in the kitchen. Load your food, set the delay timer to come on when you want it to and walk away. The delayed timer will cook your food and have it ready when you need it. You can't get much more convenient than that.

*Trapped in Flavor*

You already read how the pressure cooker seals in nutrients. However, the same process also seals in the flavor of your favorite, and not so favorite, foods. The pot is completely sealed which means the nutrients and aroma both stay in the pot, and in the food rather than being spread around the house. Fish, meat, fruits and veggies all retain their original juice and you'll enjoy the flavorful benefits.

*Tasty and Tender*

The IP cooks up meat and bones and makes them tender. When the cooking time has completed, the bones will separate from the tender meat. While cooking under pressure, whole grains and beans are softer and more flavorful than when they are cooked using other methods.

*Energy Efficient*

The Instant Pot is considered a "green" appliance because it saves as much as 70% electricity when compared to other cooking appliances. There is a good reason the Instant Pot cooks so efficiently. It was designed that way. There features ensure the IP works efficiently.

- Food cooks faster when it is under pressure and high temperature. Less cooking time equates to consuming less energy.
- The exterior portion of the IP is fully insulated. It's made up of two layers of air pockets situated between the inner pot and the outside of the pot. It's cool to touch and gets only lukewarm when it cooks for long periods of time.
- The IP has an intelligent monitoring system. This means it only heats to a certain pressure level. When cooking something for a long time, heating will be off about 40% of the total cooking time.
- The unique sealing feature of the IP requires less water to be used. This reduces the heat the IP puts off, which means your kitchen doesn't get all hot and steamy when cooking during the summer months.

## Unique Safety Features

Conventional stove-top pressure cooker disasters were because of user error. However, the new Instant Pot is designed so that most potential problems are avoided or eliminated altogether. Instant Pot is manufactured by the leading manufacturer of pressure cookers. They have already put 10 million in households around the globe.

Stove-top pressure cookers use a weighted regulator on the lid to help maintain pressure. The Instant Pot uses a patented sensor which is more precise and automated. When the inside pressure builds, the bottom of the pot, called the flat, flexible board, shifts downward and triggers the pressure sensor. It moves back up as the pressure releases. The sensor controls the heating element to help keep the pressure inside a safe range.

There are 10 safety features built in to the Instant Pot.

1- Lid Close Detection – if the lid is not properly closed, the functions will not work.
2- Leaky Lid Protection – if the cooker lid leaks, the cooker will not function. It will not heat to the pre-set pressure level. The pot can sense when the pre-heating time is not right. If it takes too long to heat up, the pot will switch to keep warm, so food doesn't burn.
3- Lid-Lock – The lid will remain locked as long as the cooker is holding pressure.
4- Vent for Anti-blockage – When food is cooking, it could jam the steam release vent. There is a special shield protecting the vent from becoming blocked.
5- Temperature Control – A built-in thermostat regulates the temperature of the inner pot to ensure it stays in a safe range for the foods being cooked.
6- High Temp Warnings – Pressure will not operate if there is no water or moisture inside. To avoid overheating, the IP will stop heating after the temp reaches a certain limit.
7- Power Shut-off – If the pot reaches too high of a temperature, it will shut off automatically.
8- Automated Pressure Controls - A sensor mechanism keeps the pressure at the right psi.

9- Regulating Pressure – If the pressure exceeds 15.23 psi, it will automatically start to release steam to bring down the pressure in the pot.

10- Excessive Pressure – If the pressure reaches an extreme level and the pressure regulator fails to function, it will activate the internal protection mechanism. This creates a gap between the lid and inner pot to which steam is released. This stops the heating and releases pressure.

# Ketogenic Instant Pot Recipes

## Instant Pot Ketogenic Breakfast Recipes

### *Keto Egg Cups on the Go*

Per Serving: Fat 9g/ Protein 9g/ Carbs 2g

**Ingredients:**

- 4 large eggs
- 1 cup of diced veggies of your choice (onions, tomatoes, mushrooms, bell peppers, jalapeno peppers)
- ½ cup sharp cheddar cheese, shredded
- ¼ cup half-and-half
- Salt and pepper to preferences
- 2 Tbsp. cilantro, chopped (or any other herb)
- For topping: ½ cup shredded cheese

**Instructions:**

1. Mix all the ingredients together in a bowl. Divide between four ½ pint wide mouth jars. Place the lids loosely on top, but do not tighten them. This just keeps the water out of the egg mixture.
2. Put 2 cups of water into the Instant Pot and then place the trivet inside.
3. Place the jars with the egg mixture on the trivet.
4. Cook for 5 minutes at high pressure. (Press "+" until the display says 5. Then push start)
5. Instantly release the steam when the beeper indicates the cooking cycle is complete.
6. Carefully remove jars, top eggs with the remaining cheese.
7. Place in an air fryer or broil for 2 to 3 minutes to brown the cheese on top if desired.

# *Boiled Eggs in the Instant Pot*

Per Egg: Fat 5g/ Protein 6g/ Carbs 0g

## Ingredients:

- 16 large eggs
- 1 cup of water

## Instructions:

1. Place the wire rack in the bottom of the Instant Pot and add the cup of water.
2. Place the raw eggs on top of the rack and fit them in tightly. May be able to get in as many as 16, but it will depend on the size of the eggs.
3. Put the lid on the Instant Pot and make sure the valve is closed. Press "+" until the display shows 4. Press "start".
4. When the timer beeps indicating cooking cycle has ended, press cancel. Manually release pressure. If you leave the eggs in the pot they will over cook.
5. Carefully move the eggs to a large bowl and cover with cold water and let them set for about 5 minutes.
6. Peel the eggs while they are still warm.
7. Eat immediately, or store in the refrigerator.

# *Coconut Milk Yogurt*

Per Serving: Fat 14g/ Protein 1g/ Carbs 2g

## Ingredients:

- 33.8 fl. oz. container of Coconut Cream
- 2 caps probiotic (xymogen Probiomax DF Probiotic)

## Instructions:

1. Empty one of the probiotic capsules into a quart-sized mason jar. Then divide the coconut cream between the two jars evenly. Cap the jars with sterile lids and shake well to combine the ingredients. Remove the lids.
2. Place the two jars (with no lids) into the stainless-steel insert for the IP cooker. Seal the top and close the vent.
3. Press "yogurt" button and set the timer to 12 hours.
4. After 12 hours, take the jars out of the IP. Refrigerate, uncovered for at least 12 more hours before eating. After the additional 12 hours place a lid on the jar for storing in the refrigerator.

# Sous Vide Bacon Egg Bites "Starbucks" Style

Per Serving: Fat 8g/ Protein 9g/ Carbs 3g (net)

## Ingredients:

- 4 eggs
- ¼ cup of egg whites
- 4 bacon slices (cooked and crumbled)
- ½ cup cottage cheese
- ¼ cup whipping cream (heavy)
- ½ chopped red pepper
- ½ chopped green pepper
- 1 cup chopped purple onion
- 1 cup shredded cheese of your choice
- Salt/pepper to preference
- 1 cup water for the Instant Pot

You will also need the silicon baby food container for use in the Instant Pot.

## Instructions:

1. Put eggs, egg whites, cottage cheese, cream, shredded cheese, and salt and pepper into a blender and blend for 30 to 45 seconds. Just until blended well.
2. Put the cup of water in the Instant Pot and place the trivet inside.
3. Add the baby food container.
4. Using a ladle, carefully fill the compartments with the egg mixture.
5. Top off with bacon, onions and chopped peppers.
6. Cover with the baby container lid, making sure the egg bites are covered. Then place the lid on the Instant pot and seal it.

7. Use the steam function and set the timer for 12 minutes. Do not do an immediate release when the timer is done. Allow it to release naturally for 10 minutes, then release the steam.

8. Remove the container and allow the egg bites to cool for several minutes.

9. Remove the egg bites by carefully pressing up on the bottom of each compartment. They should slide right out. Enjoy!

# *Keto Poblano Cheese Frittata*

Per Serving: Fat 19g/ Protein 14g/ Carbs 6g

## Ingredients:

- 4 eggs
- 1 cup of half-and-half
- 1 (10-oz.) can green chilies
- ½ tsp. salt
- ½ tsp. cumin
- 1 cup shredded cheese
- ¼ cup cilantro (chopped)

## Instructions:

1. Beat eggs, then stir in half and half, green chilies, salt to taste, cumin and 1.2 cup of the shredded cheese.
2. Pour egg mixture into a silicone pan, or a 6-inch well-greased metal pan. You can use glass, but it will take longer to cook.
3. Put 2 cups of water in the Instant Pot and put the trivet inside. Put the covered silicone pan on top of the trivet.
4. Use the "+" to set the pressure cooker to cook on high for 20 minutes. When it is done, let the steam release on its own for 10 minutes. Then, let the rest of the steam out.
5. Sprinkle the other half cup of cheese on the top of the quiche. Broil it for 5 minutes to brown and melt the cheese.

# *Spinach, Tomato and Feta Egg Cups*

Per Serving: Fat 25g/ protein 65g/ Carbs 2.7g

## Ingredients:

- 1 cup of chopped baby spinach
- ¼ cup feta cheese
- 1 Roma tomato chopped
- ½ cup mozzarella cheese
- 6 eggs
- 1 cup of water
- ½ tsp. salt
- 1 tsp. pepper

## Instructions:

1. Pour the cup of water in the bottom of the Instant Pot, then place the trivet inside.
2. Split the chopped spinach between the cups.
3. In a bowl, mix the rest of the ingredients and beat until the eggs mix in well.
4. Pour the mixture into the cups. Leave about a ¼ of an inch at the top of each cup.
5. Press the "manual" button and set to cook on high pressure for 8 minutes. Manually release the pressure as soon as they are done.

# *Mini-Mushroom Quiche*

Per Serving: Fat 13.g/ Protein 11.8g/ Carbs 2.6g

## Ingredients:

- 3 oz. of shredded Swiss cheese
- 2 oz. of finely chopped Cremini mushrooms
- 1 chopped scallion
- 4 eggs
- ¼ cup of heavy cream
- ½ tsp. salt
- 1 cup water

## Instructions:

1. Using the silicone "egg bites" mold, press the Swiss cheese firmly into the bottom of the mold. It should slightly go up the sides. Divide out the mushrooms evenly to place some in each cup on top of the Swiss cheese. Top them off with the chopped scallions.

2. Put the eggs, cream, and salt in a blender and mix well. Pour this mixture over the cheese and mushrooms.

3. Put a cup of water in the bottom of the Instant Pot and put the trivet inside. Place the silicone tray on top of the trivet.

4. Put the lid on the IP, seal it and close the pressure valve. Press "manual" and set the IP to cook at high pressure for 5 minutes and press start. When it beeps, wait 5 minutes while it releases steam naturally. Then release the remaining pressure.

5. Remove the silicone tray and turn it over to remove the mini quiches. Then turn the quiches back over so the mushrooms are on the top and the cheese crust is the bottom.

# Instant Pot Ketogenic Soup and Stew Recipes

## *Jalapeno Popper Soup*

Per Serving: Fat 40.1 g/ Protein 41.2 g/ Carbs 3.4g

### Ingredients:

- 1.5 lbs. boneless, skinless chicken breasts (cubed)
- 3 Tbsp. butter
- 2 cloves of minced garlic
- ½ chopped onion
- ½ chopped green bell pepper
- 2 whole jalapenos (seeded, chopped)
- ½ lb. of cooked, crumbled bacon
- 6 oz. cream cheese
- 3 cups chicken broth
- 1 cup whipping cream
- ¼ tsp. paprika
- 1 tsp. cumin
- 1 tsp. salt
- ½ tsp. black pepper
- ¾ cup each: Monterrey Jack and Cheddar Cheese
- ½ tsp. xanthan gum

### Instructions:

1. Press the sauté or brown button on the Instant Pot then add butter, onions, bell pepper and jalapeno peppers and the powdered spices. Continue to sauté until onions become translucent.
2. Add broth, cream cheese and cubed chicken.

3. Set the Instant Pot to cook on manual for 15 minutes. (Remember it will take a few minutes for the pot to build pressure and then the timer will start counting down.)

4. Once the cycle has finished, allow for 5 minutes of natural release. Then manually, carefully release the steam.

5. Turn the Instant Pot sauté setting on.

6. Remove the chunks of chicken and use forks to shred it, then return it to the pot.

7. Add whipping cream, both cheeses and bacon. Stir just until cheeses are melted.

8. Sprinkle the xanthan gum on the top to provide thickening. Turn on the warm setting.

9. Let the soup simmer for a little while so soup will thicken.

10. Option – serve with grated cheese, bacon or jalapenos sprinkled on top.

# *Unstuffed Cabbage Soup*

Per Serving – Fat: 14.8g/ Protein: 15.6g/ Carbs: 6.4g (4.3 net carbs minus 2.1g fiber)

## Ingredients:

- ½ onion diced
- 2 cloves of garlic minced
- 1.5 lbs. ground beef
- 3 cups of beef broth
- 1 (14 oz.) can of diced tomatoes
- 1 (8 oz.) can of tomato sauce
- ¼ cup Bragg's Aminos
- 1 small to medium head of cabbage (chopped)
- 3 tsp. Worcestershire Sauce
- ¼ tsp. parsley
- ½ tsp. salt
- ½ tsp. black pepper

## Instructions:

1. Using the Instant Pot sauté setting, brown the beef, onions and garlic. Once it is browned, drain it, then put it back in the Instant Pot.
2. Add all the other ingredients to the meat in the pot.
3. Place the lid and lock into position. Turn off sauté feature by pressing off or stop button. Press "soup."
4. Allow the IP to complete its soup cycle, then do a quick release of the steam.
5. Enjoy!

*easy to make — very tasty!*

## Low Carb Taco Soup

Per 2 Cup serving: Fat 28g/ Protein 27g/ Carbs 8g

### Ingredients:

- 2 lbs. ground beef
- 1 Tbsp. onion flakes (optional)
- 4 cloves of garlic (minced)
- 2 Tbsp. chili powder
- 2 tsp. cumin
- 8 oz. of cream cheese
- 20 oz. diced tomatoes with chilies
- 32 oz. beef broth
- ½ cup cream (heavy)
- Salt and pepper to taste preference

*Optional Toppings:*

- Sour cream
- Jalapeno peppers
- Cheddar cheese

### Instructions:

1. Turn the sauté function on the Instant Pot to on and brown the ground meat. If needed, drain the extra grease.
2. Stir in garlic, chili powder, cumin, tomatoes, beef broth, and salt and pepper.
3. Place the lid on the Instant Pot and press "soup" function setting it for 5 minutes.
4. After the soup has cooked, do not release the steam. Let it set for a about 10 more minutes before releasing the steam.
5. Stir in the heavy cream and cream cheese.
6. Serve hot with additional toppings of your choice.

# *Jalapeno Cheeseburger Spicy Soup*

Per Serving: Fat 18.3g/ Protein 16.9g/ Carbs 5.9g

## Ingredients:

- 3 bacon strips (chopped)
- 1 lb. ground beef
- ½ cup diced onions
- 1 cup diced tomatoes (with the liquid)
- ½ red bell pepper
- ½ orange bell pepper
- ½ yellow bell pepper
- ½ jalapeno pepper (deseeded and minced)
- 4 cups of beef broth
- 1 tsp. salt
- ½ tsp. minced garlic
- ½ tsp. black pepper
- 1 Tbsp. tomato paste
- 2/3 cup coconut milk
- Shredded cheese to use for topping

## Instructions:

1. Using the sauté button, fry the bacon. Once the bacon is done, remove and set aside.
2. Add onions to the bacon grease and sauté until slightly translucent. Add the ground beef and cook until totally brown. Press the "cancel" button to stop cooking.
3. Add tomatoes, all the peppers, beef broth, salt, garlic, black pepper and tomato paste. Stir until it is well combined.

4. Place the lid in place and make sure the valve is closed. Press the "soup" button and set it for 10 minutes.

5. Once the cooking cycle is complete, manually release the steam. Add the coconut milk and stir. Top each serving off with cheese and a little bit of crumbled bacon.

# *Cabbage-Beef Soup*

Per Serving: Fat 18g/ Protein 17g/ Carbs 6g

## Ingredients:

- 2 lbs. of ground beef
- ¼ onion – diced
- 1 clove of garlic – minced
- 1 tsp. cumin
- 1 head cabbage – chopped
- 4 cups beef stock
- 10 oz. can diced tomatoes with green chilies
- Salt and pepper to taste

## Instructions:

1. Brown ground beef either in the Instant Pot using the "brown" setting or precook it prior to making the soup.
2. Place all the ingredients in the Instant Pot, including the browned beef.
3. Place the lid on the IP and lock in place. Make sure the valve is set to seal.
4. Press the "soup" setting and set it for 35 minutes.
5. Let the steam release naturally.

# *Creamy Chicken-Bacon Chowder*

Per Serving: Fat: 32g/ Protein: 15.9g/ Carbs: 5.3g

## Ingredients:

- 6 boneless chicken thighs
- 8 oz. full fat cream cheese
- 3 cloves garlic (minced)
- 1 cup onion/celery mixed (fresh or frozen)
- 6 oz. mushrooms (sliced)
- 4 Tbsp. butter
- 1 tsp. thyme
- Pepper and salt to taste preference
- 3 cups chicken broth
- 1 cup heavy cream
- 1 lb. cooked and chopped bacon
- 2 cups fresh spinach

## Instructions:

1. Cut up the chicken thighs into small pieces, cubes work well. Place the chicken, cream cheese, garlic, onion and celery mix, mushrooms, butter, thyme and salt and pepper in a zipper bag. Store it until you are ready to cook.
2. When you are ready to cook the chicken, pour the chicken mixture in the IP. Add chicken broth and cook for 30 minutes using the "soup" setting.
3. Stir the chicken mixture, then add cream and spinach and mix well. Cover the Instant Pot and let it set for 10 minutes. This will let the spinach wilt.
4. Cover with chopped bacon and enjoy!

# *Loaded Cauliflower Soup*

Per Serving: Fat: 25g/ Protein: 18g/ Carbs:8g

## Ingredients:

- ½ onion
- 2 Tbsp. oil of your choice
- 1 head of cauliflower
- 3 cups chicken stock (homemade is best)
- 1 clove garlic crushed
- 1 tsp. salt/ground black pepper to taste
- 4 oz. cream cheese
- 1 cup grated sharp cheddar cheese
- ½ cup heavy cream

*Toppings:*

- Extra sharp cheddar cheese
- 8-10 strips cooked and crumbled bacon
- Chopped green onions

## Instructions:

1. Finely chop the onion. Remove leaves and stem from the cauliflower head. You can keep the stem but chop it up into small pieces.
2. Turn the Instant Pot sauté feature on and heat the oil. Add onions and garlic and sauté for just a couple of minutes. Add the cauliflower, chicken stock, and salt. Lock the lid and use the manual setting to cook on high pressure for five minutes. Use the quick release method to release the steam when it's done.
3. While the soup is cooking, cut the cream cheese into cubes, grate the cheddar cheese and cook the bacon. Crumble the bacon up after it has cooked. Cut up any other topping you want to use such as green onions.

4. Blend the soup in a food processor or immersion blender. Be careful, since it is still hot. If you want it thinner, add more stock. If you want it to thicken, let it simmer a little while longer.

5. Add the cream cheese cubes and grated cheese. Stir until the cheeses are melted in good. Then add the heavy cream. Season with salt and pepper as desired.

6. Serve hot with bacon and other preferred toppings.

# *Buffalo Chicken Soup*

Per Serving – Fat: 16g/ Protein: 27g/ Carbs: 4g

## Ingredients:

- 1 Tbsp. Olive oil (or oil of your choice)
- ½ of a large onion (chopped)
- ½ cup diced celery
- 4 minced garlic cloves
- 1 lb. of cooked, shredded chicken
- 4 cups chicken broth or bone broth
- 3 Tbsp. buffalo sauce (check label – no sugar)
- 6 oz. cream cheese cubed
- ½ cup heavy cream

## Instructions:

1. Turn on the sauté feature on the IP and add the oil, onion and celery. Sauté for about five to 10 minutes stirring occasionally.
2. Add the garlic and sauté for just about a minute more, then turn the IP off.
3. Add the chicken, broth of your choice and buffalo sauce.
4. Cover and seal the IP. Press the Soup button and set for 5 minutes. Let the pressure release for five minutes when it is done, then quick release.
5. Carefully ladle the liquid portion out of the Instant Pot and put it into a blender. Add the cubed cheese and puree until it is smooth. If it's too thick, add more liquid.
6. Pour the mixture back into the chicken in the Instant Pot. Add the cream and stir.
7. Enjoy!

# *Italian Sausage Kale Soup*

Per Serving – Fat: 33g/ Protein: 16g/ Carbs: 8g

## Ingredients:

- Cup of diced onion
- 6 minced gloves of garlic
- 1 pound ground Italian sausage
- 12 ounces frozen (or fresh) cauliflower
- 12 ounces frozen (or fresh) kale
- 3 cups of water
- ½ cup heavy cream
- ½ cup shredded Parmesan cheese

## Instructions:

1. Turn the Instant Pot on sauté.
2. Once it is hot, add the sausage and break it down with a spoon.
3. Add garlic and onion. You are not cooking the sausage – the Instant Pot will do that. Just mix it all together for now.
4. Add frozen kale and cauliflower.
5. Pour in the three cups of water. Close and seal the IP.
6. Set to cook on high for 3 minutes. Let the pressure release naturally for five minutes once it is done. Then use instant release.
7. Open the IP and stir. Add the whipping cream and mix. You can also mash cauliflower at this point. That will make the soup thicker.
8. Pour into bowls and add Parmesan cheese garnish.
9. Enjoy!

# *Egg Roll Soup*

Per Serving – Fat 9g/ Protein: 36.3g/ Carbs 13g

## Ingredients:

- 1 Tbsp. avocado oil, olive oil, or ghee
- 1 lb. of ground pastured pork
- 1 large diced onion
- 4 cups chicken, beef or veggie broth
- ½ head of cabbage – chopped
- 2 cups carrots shredded
- 1 tsp. garlic powder
- 1 tsp. onion powder
- 1 tsp. salt
- 1 tsp. ginger
- 2/3 cup coconut aminos

## Instructions:

1. Using the sauté function on your Instant Pot, brown the pork and onions in the fat of your choice. Cook until there is no pink showing in the meat.
2. Add all the rest of the ingredients. Using the manual button, set the IP to cook on high pressure for 25 minutes. When it is done, release using quick release method.
3. Remove the lid and serve.

# *Easy Broccoli Cheddar Soup*

Per Serving: Fat 35.4g/ Protein 17.5g/ Carbs 8.2g

## Ingredients:

- 1 tsp. butter
- 3 cloves of garlic, minced
- 3 ½ cups veggie broth
- 3 cups chopped broccoli
- 1 cup heavy whipping cream
- 3 cups shredded cheddar cheese
- 2 slices of bacon cooked and chopped
- Salt and pepper to taste

## Instructions:

1. Press the sauté button on the Instant Pot. Add garlic and cook about 2 minutes until it is softened. Add the veggie broth, cream, and broccoli. Use the soup setting to cook on high pressure for 3 minutes.

2. Allow the steam to release for 2 minutes naturally, then do a quick release to allow the rest of the steam to escape quickly. Remove from the instant pot and add cheese. Stir constantly until the cheese is totally melted. Then stir in the bacon. Season with salt and pepper as desired.

# *Zuppa Toscana Soup*

Per Serving – Fat: 19g/ Protein: 14g/ Carbs: 7g

## Ingredients:

- 1 lb. of ground Italian sausage (hot or mild per your preference)
- 1 Tbsp. avocado or olive oil
- ½ cup onion diced finely
- 36 oz. of chicken or vegetable broth
- Large head of cauliflower – broken into small florets
- 3 cups of chopped kale
- ¼ tsp. crushed red pepper flakes
- 1 tsp. salt
- ½ tsp. pepper
- ½ cup heavy cream

## Instructions:

1. Using the sauté setting on the Instant Pot, brown the Italian sausage until it is fully cooked. Turn the IP off and then remove the sausage and discard any oil. Clean the pot out and wipe it out with a paper towel.
2. Turn the Instant Pot back on by pushing the sauté button. Add your choice of oil and the onions. Sauté them for 3 or 4 minutes, until they are translucent in appearance. Add the sausage, chicken or vegetable broth, cauliflower, kale, red peppers, salt and pepper to the Instant Pot. Mix well.
3. Set the IP to cook on high pressure for 5 minutes. When the cycle ends, let it release naturally for 10 minutes. Do a quick release to let the rest of the steam escape. Add the cream, mix well and serve hot.

# Instant Pot Ketogenic Meat Recipes

## *Balsamic Pot Roast*

Per Serving – Fat: 28g/ Protein: 30g/ Carbs: 3g

**Ingredients:**

- About 3 lbs. of boneless chuck roast
- 1 Tbsp. kosher salt
- 1 tsp. ground black pepper
- 1 tsp. garlic powder
- ¼ cup balsamic vinegar
- 2 cups of water
- ½ cup chopped onion
- ¼ tsp. xanthan gum
- Chopped fresh parsley for garnish

**Instructions:**

1. Cut the roast into two pieces and season it with the salt, black pepper and garlic powder. Make sure to get the seasonings on both sides.
2. Use the sauté button on the Instant Pot and brown both pieces of the roast on both sides.
3. Once the meat is browned, add the vinegar, water and onion. Seal the lid on the IP.
4. Set the manual pressure cooker timer to 35 minutes. Once the timer goes off, release the pressure to let it vent manually. Then remove the lid.
5. Take the meat out of the pan and place it in a large bowl.
6. Using the sauté/brown button bring the liquid left in the IP to a boil. Let it simmer for about 10 minutes. (It will cook down.)
7. Whisk in the xanthan gum. Put the meat back in the pan and stir.
8. Turn off the IP.
9. Serve the roast mixture hot – over cauliflower and garnish with fresh parsley.

# *Smothered Pork Chops*

Per Serving – Fat: 32.61g/ Protein: 14.75g/ Carbs 4.06g

## Ingredients:

- 4 boneless pork loin chops (4 to 6 oz. each)
- 1 Tbsp. paprika
- 1 tsp. garlic powder
- 1 tsp. onion powder
- 1 tsp. pepper
- 1 tsp. salt
- ¼ tsp. cayenne pepper
- 2 Tbsp. coconut oil
- ½ onion (sliced)
- 6 oz. baby bella mushrooms
- 1 Tbsp. butter
- ½ cup cream (heavy cream)
- ¼ to ½ tsp. xanthan gum
- 1 Tbsp. fresh parsley (chopped)

## Instructions:

1. Mix together in a small bowl: paprika, garlic and onion powder, salt and pepper, and cayenne pepper.
2. Rinse off the pork chops and pat dry.
3. Sprinkle one tablespoon of spice mixture on both sides of each pork chop. Rub the seasoning into the meat. Set the extra spices aside.
4. Heat coconut oil in the Instant Pot using the Sauté setting. Brown the porkchops, then remove them to a plate. Turn off the IP.

5. Add onions and mushrooms to the bottom of the Instant Pot. Place the pork chops on top.

6. Add the lid and seal. Cook on manual high setting for 25 minutes. Once the cooking has completed you can either do an immediate release, or let it release slowly.

7. After the steam has been released, remove the lid and put the pork chops on a serving plate. Leave the other mixture in the pot.

8. Press sauté and add the remaining spice mixture, butter, and cream into the hot liquid. Whisk it all together.

9. Sprinkle the xanthan gum into the cooking liquid and whisk. Let it simmer for 3 to 5 minutes, until the sauce is thick, and the butter is melted. Turn the pot off. Add more xanthan gum until the gravy is your preferred consistency.

10. Top off the pork chops with the mushroom and onion gravy. Sprinkle with fresh parsley and enjoy!

# *Italian Meatballs*

Per Serving of 3 meatballs and ½ cup sauce – Fat: 33g/ Protein: 34g/ Carbs: 5g (net)

## Ingredients:

- 1 and ½ lbs. ground beef
- 2 Tbsp. chopped, fresh parsley
- ¾ cup Parmesan cheese (grated)
- ½ cup almond flour
- 2 medium eggs
- 1 tsp. salt
- ¼ tsp. black pepper
- ¼ tsp. garlic powder
- 1 tsp. dried onion flakes
- ¼ tsp. dried oregano
- 1/3 cup water (warm)

*To cook meatballs:*

- 1 tsp. olive oil or avocado oil
- 3 cups keto marinara sauce (or sugar free marinara sauce)
- 

## Instructions:

1. Combine all the ingredients for the meatballs in a large bowl and mix well. Then form it into about 15 meatballs.
2. Put the oil in the bottom of the Instant Pot and brown then using the sauté function. Once they are browned, layer them on the bottom of the pot, leaving about ½ inch between them. (Don't press them down.)
3. Pour the marinara sauce of the meatballs, then seal the lid according to the instructions that came with your pot.
4. Set the Instant pot to low pressure to cook for 10 minutes.
5. After the timer indicates the cycle is done, open the valve so the steam can escape.
6. Remove the lid and serve meatballs over spaghetti squash or zoodles.

*Super-easy prep if you buy the bacon pieces pre-done 50-50.*

# Chicken Crack!

*I think it's pretty good.*
*Erik loves it.*

Per Serving – Fat: 28.4g/ Protein: 41.1g/ Carbs: 3.5g

## Ingredients:

- 2 lbs. chicken breast
- 12 oz. of cream cheese
- 2 packs of dry Ranch Dressing Mix (make your own – recipe below)
- 8 oz. cooked, crumbled bacon  *not too much*
- ½ cup cheddar cheese
- 1 cup of bone broth (can use water)

*Keto Friendly "Dry Ranch" Recipe:*

- ½ cup dry buttermilk powder (can leave this out!)
- 1 Tbsp. dry parsley
- 2 tsp. dry dill
- 1 tsp. chives
- 1 Tbsp. garlic powder
- 1 Tbsp. onion powder
- 1 tsp. salt
- ½ tsp. black pepper

## Instructions:

1. Pour the cup of bone broth, broth or water into the Instant Pot and add the chicken.
2. Cut up the cream cheese and place the cubes on top of the chicken. Add the seasonings on top of the cream cheese.
3. Set the pressure cooker on high for 12 minutes.
4. When it's done, do a quick release.
5. Remove the chicken and shred it.
6. Put the chicken back in the IP with the remaining juices. Add cheddar cheese and bacon then mix it all together.
7. Put the lid back on the pot, and let it set for about 5 minutes to let the cheese melt.
8. Serve and enjoy!

# *Jamaican Jerk Roast*

Per Serving – Fat: 20g/ Protein: 23g/ Carbs: 0g

## Ingredients:

- 4 lbs. pork shoulder roast
- ¼ cup Jamaican Jerk spice with no MSG or sugar (Badia Brand)
- 1 Tbsp. olive oil or avocado oil
- ½ cup beef stock or broth

## Instructions:

1. Rub the shoulder roast with the oil of your choice and the Jamaican Jerk spices.
2. Use the sauté or brown setting on your Instant Pot to sear the roast an all sides.
3. Add the beef stock or broth.
4. Close and seal the Instant Pot and set it to cook for 45 minutes on high pressure.
5. Release pressure according to the instructions in your booklet.
6. Shred the roast and serve alongside your favorite sides.

# *Italian Braised Chicken*

Per Serving – Fat: 7.5g/ Protein: 29.5g/ Carbs 6g

## Ingredients:

- 10 chicken thighs (about 5 ounces each)
- Salt and pepper to taste
- 3 to 4 sprigs of fresh rosemary
- 1 TBL plus 1 tsp olive oil
- Large yellow onion chopped
- Celery stock
- Carrot
- Red pepper flakes (optional)
- 2 cups crushed tomatoes
- ¼ tsp marjoram (dried)
- ¼ cup dry white wine (can be omitted)
- 2 cups chicken broth or vegetable broth

## Instructions:

1. Sprinkle a little salt and pepper on the chicken to your taste preference. Press the sauté button on the Instant Pot and put ½ tablespoon of oil in. Brown and sear the half the chicken on all sides. It should take about 5 to 7 minutes on each site. Remove the chicken and set aside. Then do the same with the rest of the chicken.
2. Add the rest of the oil, onions, garlic, carrots, celery and red peppers if you are using them. Cook on sauté for about 3 or 4 minutes, just until they are soft. Add the wine and chicken broth.
3. Add the tomatoes, marjoram and salt and pepper to taste. Put all the chicken in the sauce.
4. Close the lid and seal. Set the IP to cook on high pressure for 30 minutes, then allow it to release naturally.

# *Bolognese for the Instant Pot*

Per Serving – Fat: 5g/ Protein: 12g/ Carbs 7g

## Ingredients:

- 4 oz. center cut bacon, or pancetta (chopped)
- 1 Tbsp. unsalted butter
- 1 minced white onion
- 2 stalks celery minced
- 2 carrots minced
- 2 lbs. of ground beef
- ¼ cup dry white wine
- 2 (2 oz.) cans crushed tomatoes    $2x$ (28 oz) cans
- 3 bay leaves
- Salt and pepper to taste
- ½ cup cream (or half & Half)
- ¼ cup fresh parsley

## Instructions:

1. Using the sauté setting, brown the pancetta until the fat melts or about 4 to 5 minutes.
2. Add butter, onion, carrot and celery and cook until they are soft. This will take about 6 to 8 minutes.
3. Add the ground meat and add salt and pepper to taste. Sauté it until the meat is browned.
4. Add the wine and let it cook down for 3 or 4 minutes.
5. Add the tomatoes, bay leaves, salt and pepper. Set the Instant Pot to cook at high pressure for 15 minutes.
6. Let the steam release naturally. Then open the pot and stir in the cream. Add parsley as a garnish and serve over spaghetti squash or zoodles.

or Spaghetti style shirataki noodles
Zoodles
or over raw cole slaw / lettuce

# *Barbacoa (Chipotle Copy)*

Per Serving – Fat: 28.4g/ Protein: 23.4g/ Cars 4.8g

## Ingredients:

- 2-3 lbs. beef chuck roast
- 1 cup of beef broth
- Juice of a small lime
- 1/3 cup apple cider vinegar
- 3 bay leaves
- 3 chipotle peppers – canned in adobo (save the juice)
- 2 Tbsp. olive oil, bacon fat, or avocado oil
- 1 ½ Tbsp. cumin
- 1 tsp. pepper
- 1 Tbsp. salt (to taste)
- 1 Tbsp. tomato paste
- 2 tsp. oregano
- 1 tsp. cinnamon
- 1 tsp. onion powder
- ¼ tsp. ground cloves

## Instructions:

1. Prepare the roast by seasoning all the sides with salt and pepper. Cut off any unwanted fat (if you think it'll be too chewy.)
2. Put the bacon fat or olive oil in the IP and then add the beef. Sear it on every side.
3. Put the lime juice, vinegar, chipotle peppers, adobo, cumin, pepper, salt, tomato paste, cinnamon, onion powder, and cloves in a blender and blend until smooth.
4. After the roast has browned, cover it with the spice puree. Add bay leaves and broth.

5.  Close the lid and seal it. Then use the Manual button to set the roast to cook for 50 minutes on high pressure.

6.  Once the timer ends, turn off the Pot and let the pressure come down by itself. This may take about 20 minutes, but it will make it tender.

7.  Remove from the Instant Pot and shred. Then, return it to the liquid and serve with cauliflower rice.

# *Orange Turkey*

Per Serving – Fat: 1.3g/ Protein: 12.2g/ Carbs: 10.5g

## Ingredients:

- 3 oranges
- 8 oz. of turkey breasts
- 1 onion
- 2 Tbsp. your choice of no or low-carb sweetener (Stevia)
- 1 Tbsp. Thyme
- 1 Tbsp. basil
- 1 tsp. paprika
- 1 tsp. celery salt
- Salt and pepper

## Instructions:

1. Make your marinade by grating the three oranges and setting the zest aside. Then juice the oranges into a bowl. Add all the seasoning and sweetener to the juice and mix well.
2. Clean and dice the onion and set it aside.
3. Dice the turnkey breasts and put it in the marinade. Mix it well and place it in the fridge to set for an hour.
4. Lay down a piece of aluminum foil and use a slotted spoon to remove the turkey from the marinade. Put the turkey on the aluminum foil and add a tiny bit of the juice on it. Seal the foil around the turkey to make sort of a pocket.
5. Put one cup of water in the Instant Pot and then put the steam basket inside. Then place the foil with the turkey on top of the steamer.

6. Use the poultry setting on the Instant Pot and set it to cook for 8 minutes. After it is done, let it set for 2 minutes, then do a quick release to remove the rest of the pressure.

7. Carefully remove the foil and turkey and place the turkey on a plate. Place some of the orange zest and onion on top. Serve with your favorite side dish.

*tasty !*

## Low Carb Pork Ribs

Per Serving – Fat: 17.89g/ Protein: 50.55g/ Carbs: 0.25g

### Ingredients:

- 1 cup TLC low-carb BBQ sauce (or homemade – recipe below)
- 2 Tbsp. olive oil
- 3 lbs. pork side ribs
- ½ cup water or chicken stock

*BBQ Sauce Recipe:* used balsamic BBQ sauce from "The Big Book of ..."

- 2 ½ cans tomato paste (no sugar)
- ½ cup apple cider vinegar
- 1/3 cup erythritol or another sweetener
- 2 Tbsp. Worcestershire sauce
- 1 Tbsp. liquid smoke
- 2 tsp. smoked paprika
- 1 tsp. garlic powder
- ½ tsp. onion powder

used BBQ dry rub seasoning instead (Big Book ..." p. 238)

### Instructions:

1. Cut the ribs into individual pieces, then season with salt and pepper.

next time do this—
(& maybe don't leave chx stock in the pot)

2. Use the sauté function and brown the ribs in the olive oil.
3. Remove the extra oil from the Instant Pot. Use stock or water to deglaze the IP.
4. Add the ribs and half the BBQ sauce to the IP. Cook for 11 minutes using the Manual function.
5. Allow the steam to release naturally.
6. Add the other half of the BBQ sauce and toss to cover the ribs.

– added ½ cup chx stock after browning ribs. Also added ½ of BBQ sauce

# *Chicken Cacciatore*

Per Serving – Fat: 3g/ Protein: 14g/ Carbs: 10.5

## Ingredients:

- 4 chicken thighs with the bone
- Salt and pepper to taste
- Olive oil spray
- ½ can crushed tomatoes
- ½ cup diced onion
- ¼ cup diced red bell pepper
- ½ cup diced green bell pepper
- ½ tsp. dried oregano
- 1 bay leaf
- 2 Tbsp. chopped basil or chopped parsley for a topping

*Very tasty! Moderate prep.*

## Instructions:

1. Season the chicken with salt and pepper on all sides.
2. Press the sauté button on the Instant Pot. Spray it lightly with oil and then brown the chicken on both sides. When it is brown on both sides, set it aside.
3. Spray the IP with oil again, the add the onions and peppers. Sauté for about 5 minutes, or until they are soft.
4. Put the chicken back in the Instant Pot with the vegetables and pour the tomatoes over the veggies and chicken. Add the oregano and bay leaf. Add salt and pepper if desired. Stir quickly then cover and seal the lid.
5. Cook on high pressure for 25 minutes. When it is done, allow it to release naturally.
6. Remove the bay leaf, garnish with parsley and serve over spaghetti squash or cauliflower rice.

# *Garlic Chipotle Lime Chicken*

Per Serving – Fat: 9g/ Protein: 22g/ Carbs: 2g

## Ingredients:

- 1 ½ lbs. of boneless chicken breasts or thighs
- 1/3 cup tomato sauce (Check the ingredients to ensure it is sugar free.)
- 2 Tbsp. olive oil or avocado oil
- 2 to 3 cloves of garlic
- 2 Tbsp. mild green chilies (canned)
- 1 Tbsp. apple cider vinegar
- 3 Tbsp. lime juice
- 1/3 cup fresh cilantro or you can use flat leaf Italian parsley
- 1 ½ tsp. sweetener of your choice
- 1 tsp. salt
- ¼ tsp. black pepper

## Instructions:

1. Place all the ingredients except the chicken in a blender or food processor. Use the pulse button to mix until it makes a smooth sauce.
2. Put the chicken in the Instant Pot. Pour the sauce over the chicken. Then close the lid and ensure it is sealed.
3. Press the slow cooker button and cook for 4 to 6 hours on the high setting, or for 6 to 8 hours on low.
4. Serve and enjoy!

# Pot Roast with Chimichurri Sauce

Per Serving – Fat: 6.4g/ Protein: 22.2g/ Carbs: 5.7g

## Ingredients:

- 2 to 3 lbs. boneless pork roast
- 4 Tbsp. olive oil (divided out)
- 1 (1 lb.) package of carrots (trimmed and quartered)
- 1 sweet onion (sliced thick)
- Salt to taste
- Chimichurri sauce

*Chimichurri Sauce Recipe:*

- 1 cup fresh basil, parsley or cilantro leaves
- 3 garlic cloves
- ½ cup olive oil or avocado oil
- 2 Tbsp. lemon juice
- 1 tsp. salt
- ¼ tsp. black pepper
- ¼ tsp. cayenne pepper

Combine these ingredients in a food processor or a blender. Blend until the basil is evenly distributed and in small pieces.

## Instructions:

1. Turn the IP on using the sauté setting. Put 2 tablespoons of the olive oil in the pot and let it get hot. Then place the roast in and brown each side. This seals in the flavor and juices. Sprinkle a little salt and pepper on the meat as desired.

2. Turn off the sauté feature and place a cup of water in the bottom of the pot then pressure the roast on high for 45 minutes. Let the steam release naturally. This might take 25 minutes.

3. Remove the roast and set it aside. Place the carrots and onions in the Instant Pot and pressure on high for 4 minutes.

4. Then arrange the carrots and onions around the roast and drizzle with chimichurri sauce. Serve the extra sauce on the side.

**Note:** This dish can also be made using the slow cooker feature. After browning the roast, set it to cook on slow cooker mode for 6 hours on high or 8 hours on low. Do a quick release and open the lid when there is two hours of cooking time left. Add the carrots and onions then turn the Instant Pot back on the same setting for the last two hours allowing the veggies to cook.

# *Lamb Barbacoa*

Per Serving – Fat: 35.8g/ Protein: 37.5g/ Carbs: 1.2

## Ingredients:

- 5.5 lbs. boneless leg of lamb
- ¼ cup dried mustard
- 2 Tbsp. Himalayan salt
- 2 Tbsp. smoked paprika
- 1 Tbsp. ground cumin
- 1 Tbsp. dried oregano
- 1 tsp. chipotle powder
- 1 cup of water.

## Instructions:

1. Combine the spices in a small bowl and stir them so they are evenly combined. Using your hands, cover the lamb making sure to get it in all the crevices as good as you can.
2. Pour the cup of water into the IP, then place the rack in the pot and set the lamb on it.
3. Press the "meat/stew" button and set it to cook for 30 to 35 minutes depending on how well-done you prefer your meat. When it has completed cooking, let the pressure release naturally before removing the lid.
4. When the lamb is done, shred the lamb and serve as desired.

# *Chicken Tikka Masala*

Per Serving – Fat: 41.2g/ Protein: 26g/ Carbs: 5.8g

## Ingredients:

- 1 ½ lbs. of bone-in and skin-on chicken thighs
- 1 lb. of boneless and skinless chicken thighs
- 2 Tbsp. olive or avocado oil
- 2 tsp. onion powder
- 3 minced cloves of garlic
- 1-inch piece of ginger root (grated)
- 3 Tbsp. sugar-free tomato paste
- 5 tsp. garam masala
- 2 tsp. smoked paprika
- 4 tsp. salt
- 10 oz. can diced tomatoes
- 1 cup heavy cream
- 1 cup coconut milk
- Fresh cilantro for topping
- 1 tsp. guar gum

## Instructions:

1. De-bone the boned chicken thighs and then chop all the chicken into small bite-size chunks. Place the chicken in the Instant Pot and grate the 1-inch knob of ginger on top of it. Add all the dry spices to the pot. Add the diced tomatoes, oil and tomato paste on top then mix it all together until it is mixed well.

2. Add half of the coconut milk and stir again. Use the slow cooker feature and set it to cook on low for 6 hours or set it to cook on high for 3 hours.

3. When it is done, remove the lid and add the cream, the rest of the coconut milk, guar gum and stir the contents thoroughly. This should help thicken it up a bit. Serve with the side of your choosing.

# *Hot Wings*

Per Serving – Fat: 26g/ Protein: 22g/ Carbs: 3g

## Ingredients:

- 2 lbs. of chicken wings
- 1 up of hot sauce (Frank's Original)
- 3 Tbsp. lime juice
- 3 minced garlic cloves
- Salt and pepper to taste
- 1 Tbsp. avocado oil

*Ingredients for Ranch Dip:*

- 1 cup of sour cream
- ½ cup flat leaf parsley (chopped)
- 3 fresh chives (chopped)
- 1 clove garlic (minced)
- 1 tsp. dried dill
- 1 tsp. salt
- 1 tsp. black pepper
- ½ tsp. cayenne pepper
- 1 tsp. paprika

*Used these cooking directions w recipe to Easy BBQ wings from "The Big Book of Paleo Slow C."*

*- + 2 packs of wings (~24)*
*- cooked on manuel, high pressure for 7 min.*
*- naturel release steam*

## Instructions:

1. Season the chicken wings with salt and pepper. Pour the hot sauce over them. This can be made right away, but if you have time, it's best to let them marinate overnight, or at least for two hours.

2. If you don't have time to marinade, you can brown them by putting a tablespoon of oil in the Instant Pot and selecting the "sauté" mode. Add the wings to the hot oil

and sear on each side for 2 minutes. Turn off the sauté setting. Add hot sauce, lime juice and garlic to the IP.

3. If you do not want to brown the wings, marinade them, then put them in the Instant Pot with all the other ingredients at the same time.

4. Close and seal the lid on the Instant Pot. Press "manual" to set the Pot to cook for 5 minutes on high pressure. Let the pressure release naturally for at least 10 minutes before releasing the rest of the pressure and taking the lid off.

5. While the wings are in the Instant Pot cooking, mix the ranch dip up and let it chill in the fridge until you are ready to use it.

6. Serve the wings with the ranch dip. Don't forget the napkins!

# Instant Pot Ketogenic Seafood Recipes

## *Lemon & Peppered Salmon*

Per 4-oz. Serving – Fat: 16g/ Protein: 24g/ Carbs: 0

**Ingredients:**

- ¾ cup water
- A few sprigs of any combination of parsley, basil, dill, or tarragon
- 1 lb. Salmon filet
- 3 tsp. of ghee (or other healthy fat)
- ¼ tsp. salt (optional)
- ½ tsp. pepper to taste
- ½ lemon sliced thinly
- 1 red bell pepper julienned
- 1 carrot julienned

**Instructions:**

1. Put the water and herbs in the bottom of the Instant pot then put the steamer rack in place.
2. Place the salmon on the steamer rack skin side down. Drizzle the salmon with the fat of your choice, add pepper, and salt if desired. Then cover the salmon with lemon slices.
3. Close the Instant Pot making sure to seal it. Set it to steam for 3 minutes.
4. While the salmon is steaming in the IP, julienne the vegetables.
5. When the beeper indicates the steamer is done, quick release the steam. Press the cancel button to turn it off. Carefully remove salmon.
6. Remove and discard the herbs. Then put the veggies in the juices and sauté them for just a couple of minutes.
7. Serve the salmon with the vegetables. Add a teaspoon of oil, ghee or fat of your choice or pour a little of the left-over sauce on top of them if you'd like.

# *Alaskan Cod*

Per Serving – Fat: 1.6g/ Protein: 20g/ Carbs: 4g

## Ingredients:

- One large Wild Alaskan Cod fillet
- 1 cup of cherry tomatoes
- 2 Tbsp. butter
- Salt and pepper to taste
- Sprinkles of olive oil

## Instructions:

1. Choose an oven safe, glass dish that will fit inside your Instant Pot.
2. Place the tomatoes in the glass dish. Cut up the fish and place the pieces on top of the tomatoes.
3. Season with salt and pepper or any other seasonings you like on fish.
4. Top with the butter and drizzle with just a little bit of olive oil.
5. Pour one cup of water in the IP and place the trivet in the pot.
6. Set the dish inside on the trivet, close and seal the lid.
7. Push the manual, high timer for 5 minutes if the cod is thawed, or for 9 minutes if it's still frozen.
8. Release the pressure manually, once the beeper signals it's done.
9. Enjoy!

# *Salmon with Chili-Lime Sauce*

Per Serving – Fat: 25g/ Protein: 29g/ Carbs: 10.5g

## Ingredients:

*Steamed Salmon:*

- 2 salmon fillets (5 oz.)
- 1 cup water
- Salt and pepper to taste

*Chili-lime Sauce:*

- 1 jalapeno (deseeded and diced)
- Juice of one lime
- 2 minced cloves of garlic
- 1 Tbsp. honey (or other sweetener)
- 1 Tbsp. olive oil or avocado oil
- 1 Tbsp. hot water
- 1 Tbsp. fresh chopped parsley
- ½ tsp. paprika
- ½ tsp. cumin

## Instructions:

1. Combine all the ingredients for the chili-lime sauce together and set aside.
2. Add the cup of water to the Instant Pot, place the steam rack inside then place the fillets on the rack. Season the top of the fillets with salt and pepper as preferred.
3. Close and lock the lid and set to steam for 5 minutes at high pressure. Use the quick release when the cycle is done.
4. Open the pot and transfer the steamed salmon to a plate. Drizzle with the pre-made chili-lime sauce and enjoy!

# *Brazilian Fish Stew*

Per Serving – Fat: 30.2g/ Protein: 19.7g/ Carbs: 9.6g

## Ingredients:

- 1 lb. of Wild caught white fish like cod
- Juice of one lime
- 1 Tbsp. olive oil or avocado oil
- 1 jalapeno (seeds removed)
- 1 onion
- 1 red pepper
- 1 yellow pepper
- 2 cloves minced or pressed garlic
- 1 tsp. paprika
- 2 cups chicken broth
- 2 cups chopped tomatoes
- 1 tsp. salt
- ¼ tsp. black pepper
- 15 oz. coconut milk
- Chopped fresh cilantro or lime wedges for optional garnish

## Instructions:

1. Set the fillet in a bowl and add the lime juice to it so it can marinate.
2. Slice the peppers and onions then turn the Instant Pot on Sauté mode and sauté the peppers in your choice of oil. After the onions turn translucent, add the garlic.
3. Add the remaining ingredients and let it get warm.
4. Then add the fish and the lime juice. Use the timer to cook the fish stew for 3 minutes on high pressure.
5. As soon as it's done, release the steam manually. Serve the fish soup with a dash of cilantro as a garnish.

# *Keto Shrimp Scampi*

Per Serving – Fat: 14.7g/ Protein: 23.3g/ Carbs: 2.1g

## Ingredients:

- ¼ cup of chicken or vegetable broth
- ½ cup white cooking wine
- 2 Tbsp. olive or avocado oil
- 2 Tbsp. butter
- 1 Tbsp. minced garlic
- 2 Tbsp. chopped parsley
- 1 Tbsp. lemon juice
- Salt and pepper as preferred
- 1 lb. of raw peeled and deveined shrimp
- ½ tsp. red pepper flakes (optional)
- Grated parmesan for garnish (optional)

## Instructions:

1. Combine broth, wine, oil of choice, butter, garlic, parsley, lemon juice, pepper flakes and salt and pepper into the Instant Pot.
2. Add shrimp, put the lid on and seal.
3. Use the slow cooker feature and set it on low for 2 and ½ hours.
4. Enjoy!

# Asian Salmon and Vegetables

Per Serving – Fat: 17.9g/ Protein: 24.6g/ Carbs: 12.4g

## Ingredients:

- 2 salmon or other fish fillets
- 1 diced garlic clove
- 2 tsp. grated ginger
- ¼ red chili pepper diced
- Salt and pepper
- 2 Tbsp. soy sauce or gluten free tamari sauce
- 1 tsp. honey

*Vegetables:*

- ½ lb. mixed green veggies (can use cauliflower, red peppers etc. – to keep carb count down.)
- Large carrot
- Lime juice
- 1 Tbsp. tamari sauce
- 1 Tbsp. olive or avocado oil

## Instructions:

1. Put one cup of water in the Instant Pot and place a trivet or steamer rack inside.
2. Put the fillets in a heat-proof bowl or cake tin that fits in the IP. Sprinkle the fillets with garlic, ginger, red chili pepper and a little salt and pepper. Mix tamari and honey in a small bowl and pour over the fillets.
3. Put the tin or bowl in the pot, so the tin isn't touching the water. Press the manual, high pressure cooking button and set it for three minutes. While it is cooking, get the vegetables ready.
4. Cut up the veggies and put them in a steam basket and sprinkle them with garlic.

5. When the timer goes off, use the quick release method to remove pressure. The salmon will not be quite done yet.

6. Put the steam basket holding the veggies on top of the tin holding the salmon. Drizzle the lime juice, olive oil and tamari sauce on top of them. Also sprinkle with salt and pepper if desired.

7. Put the lid on, lock it in place then press the manual button again. Set the timer for 0 minutes. Yes, zero. By the time the steam builds up the veggies will be done and still a bit crunchy. When the timer goes off, wait just one minute before using quick release to let the steam off.

8. Take the veggies out and set them aside. Carefully take out the salmon and transfer it to a plate. Pour any juice on top of the salmon and serve with the veggies on the side.

*Good, not great — Flavor is a bit bland*

## Indian Shrimp Curry

Per Serving – Fat: 7.9g/ Protein: 28g/ Carbs: 10.9g

**Ingredients:**

*+ next time add mushrooms; sliced.*
*A bunch of them...* ☺

*Serve over cauliflower rice ?*

- 1 Tbsp. olive oil or avocado oil
- 1 lb. of peeled and deveined shrimp
- ½ yellow onion – chopped finely
- 1 tsp. ground ginger
- 1 tsp. ground cumin
- 1 tsp. ground coriander
- 1 ½ tsp. ground turmeric
- 1 tsp. curry powder
- 1 tsp. paprika
- ½ tsp. chili powder
- 2 garlic cloves minced
- 1 can tomato sauce (15-oz. can – no sugar added)
- ¾ cup coconut milk
- ½ tsp. salt
- Cilantro and chili peppers can be used to garnish

**Instructions:**

1. Set the Instant Pot on sauté and put 2 teaspoons of the oil of your choice in to warm. Add the shrimp and cook for one minute, just long enough to warm it a bit. Then remove it.
2. Add the other teaspoon of oil along with the onions. Sauté them for 5 minutes. Then add the ginger, cumin, coriander, turmeric, curry powder, paprika, chili powder and minced garlic. Stir well. Cook for 30 seconds then add in the tomato sauce.
3. Add in the shrimp and coconut sauce and mix well.
4. Garnish with cilantro and chili peppers.

*& coconut milk & tomato sauce*

*I skipped #1, and added the frozen (raw) shrimp in at the end of step #2 (and skipped #3 obviously). Then I did 3 mins. pressure cook (low) w quick release. It worked well - (Perhaps two minutes would have sufficed).*

# *Seafood Gumbo*

Per Serving – Fat: 10.8g/ Protein: 46.8g/ Carbs: 13.1g

## Ingredients:

- 24 oz. of sea bass filets
- 3 Tbsp. avocado oil
- 3 Tbsp. Cajun or creole seasoning
- 2 yellow onions
- 2 bell peppers
- 4 ribs of celery
- 28 oz. of diced tomatoes
- ¼ cup sugar-free tomato paste
- 3 bay leaves
- 1 ½ cups veggie broth (or chicken broth)
- 2 lbs. raw, deveined shrimp
- Salt and pepper to taste

## Instructions:

1. Cut the filets into 2-inch chunks. Evenly coat the fish pieces with salt, pepper and half of the Cajun seasoning. Set it aside.

2. Press the sauté button on the Instant Pot. Add the avocado oil to the IP and when it is warm, add the chunks of fish. Sauté for about 4 minutes or until they look cooked on all sides. Use a slotted spoon to remove the fish pieces and transfer to a plate.

3. Add onions, pepper, celery and the other half of the Cajun seasoning to the pot and sauté for about 2 minutes. Push the "keep warm" button and add the cooked fish, diced tomatoes, tomato paste, bay leaves and veggie broth. Stir.

4. Put the lid on the Instant Pot, close it and seal it. Push the manual button and set the pot to cook on high pressure for 5 minutes.

5. Once it has cooked and the Instant Pot beeps, manually release the pressure. Remove the lid then hit the sauté button again. Add the shrimp and let it cook about 3 or 4 minutes. Just until the shrimp are opaque. Add more salt and pepper if desired.

6. Serve on cauliflower rice.

# *Fish Chowder*

Per Serving – Fat: 34.4g/ Protein: 35.7g/ Carbs: 63.4g

## Ingredients:

- 4 slices of bacon (chopped)
- 1 medium onion (chopped)
- 3 cups daikon radish (chopped)
- 2 ½ cups chicken stock
- ½ tsp. dried thyme
- Salt and pepper as desired
- 2 cups heavy cream
- 1 lb. of fresh white fish (cod, pollock, tilapia)
- 1 Tbsp. butter

## Instructions:

1. Cook the bacon in the Instant Pot using the sauté function. Remove the bacon when it is crispy.
2. Add onion and radish to the leftover bacon grease and sauté until they are soft.
3. Add the chicken stock and let it simmer on the sauté setting for about 10 minutes. Season it with the thyme, salt and pepper.
4. Add the fish (chopped). Then set the IP to cook at high pressure for 5 minutes. Allow it to depressurize naturally when it is done.
5. After it has finished, add the cream and mix well. Let it continue to simmer on the keep warm setting for a few minutes until it starts getting thicker.

# Instant Pot Ketogenic Vegan Recipes

## *Butternut Squash Soup*

Per Serving – Fat: 12.9g/ Protein: 4.9g/ Carbs: 17g

**Ingredients:**

- 1 tsp. olive oil or avocado oil
- 1 large onion
- 2 garlic cloves
- 1 Tbsp. curry powder
- 1 butternut squash – peeled and cut into cubes
- 1 ½ tsp. salt
- 3 cups water
- ½ cup coconut milk

**Instructions:**

1. Turn the sauté feature on and add the olive oil and chopped up onion. Sauté until the onion is tender, then add the garlic and curry powder. Continue to sauté until it is fragrant, usually just about a minute or two.
2. Turn the IP off. Add butternut squash, salt and water. Place the lid on the Instant Pot and seal.
3. Select the "soup" setting and set the timer to cook for 30 minutes at high pressure.
4. Once the timer is done, let the steam release naturally for about 10 minutes before releasing the remaining pressure.
5. Either use an immersion blender to puree the soup in the Instant Pot or transfer the soup to a food processor or blender and blend until smooth. (Remember to use caution when blending hot foods!
6. Put the blended soup back in the Instant Pot and stir the coconut milk in. At this point you can adjust the soup's flavor for salt preference.

# *Cauliflower Mushroom Soup*

Per Serving – Fat: 2g/ Protein: 6g/ Carbs: 18g

## Ingredients:

- 1 chopped onion
- 2 tsp. olive or avocado oil
- 1 Tbsp. crushed garlic
- 1 tsp. thyme
- 1 lb. of chopped baby bella mushrooms
- 1 large head cauliflower
- 6 cups vegetable broth

## Instructions:

1. Press the sauté button on the Instant Pot and add one teaspoon of the oil of your choice. Add the onions and sauté them for about 5 minutes, or until they are brown. Add the garlic and thyme and continue to sauté for about 2 more minutes. Remove and set aside.
2. Put the other teaspoon of oil in the Instant Pot and add the chopped mushrooms. Heat them until they are lightly brown. This will take about 5 minutes and the oil should all evaporate.
3. Add the onions, cauliflower and vegetable stock to the mushrooms in the Instant Pot. Cook for 5 minutes on high pressure. Then let the pressure release naturally or you can release it manually.
4. Puree the soup using an immersion blender or put the soup in a blender to puree.
5. Enjoy!

# *Brussels Sprouts Side*

Per Serving – Fat: 8g/ Protein: 3g/ Carbs: 7g

## Ingredients:

- 2 lbs. of Brussels sprouts (halved)
- ¼ cup gluten free soy sauce
- 1 Tbsp. rice vinegar
- 2 Tbsp. sesame oil, olive oil or avocado oil
- 1 Tbsp. almonds (chopped)
- 1 tsp. red pepper flakes
- 2 tsp. garlic powder
- 1 tsp. onion powder
- 1 Tbsp. smoked paprika
- ½ tsp. cayenne pepper
- Salt and pepper as desired

## Instructions:

1. Using the sauté feature, brown the chopped almonds.
2. Add in the liquids and seasonings, then add the Brussels sprouts.
3. Set the Instant Pot to cook on high pressure for 2 minutes.
4. When it's done, do a quick, manual release. Otherwise the sprouts can become mushy.

# *Cabbage Soup*

Per Serving – Fat: 0.4g/ Protein: 2.3g/ Carbs: 13.4g

## Ingredients:

- 3 cups chopped cabbage
- 2 ½ cups vegetable broth
- 1 can diced tomatoes
- 3 chopped carrots (can reduce to cut carbs if desired)
- 3 chopped celery stalks
- 1 chopped onion
- 2 gloves garlic
- 2 Tbsp. apple cider vinegar
- 1 Tbsp. lemon juice
- 2 tsp. dried sage

## Instructions:

1. Combine all ingredients in the Instant Pot. Close the lid and seal it. Set the timer to cook at high pressure for 15 minutes. Don't worry if the cabbage makes the Pot full, it will wilt down during the cooking process.
2. When it is done cooking, allow it to release naturally. If you are in a hurry, you can release it manually, but it's best to let it release slowly as it will help blend the flavors.

# *Flavored Cauli-Rice*

Per Serving – Fat: 3.5g/ Protein: 1g/ Carbs: 2.4g

## Ingredients:

- Medium or large cauliflower
- 2 Tbsp. olive or avocado oil
- ½ tsp. parsley
- ¼ tsp. salt
- 1 cup water

*Optional Seasonings to Consider:*

- ¼ tsp. cumin
- ¼ tsp. paprika
- ¼ tsp. turmeric
- Fresh cilantro
- Lime wedges

## Instructions:

1. Wash the cauliflower head and trim the leaves. Go ahead and cut it into fourths if you'd like.
2. Put all the cauliflower into the steamer insert if your Instant Pot came with one. You can just put it in the Pot.
3. Add one cup of water to the Instant Pot, then place the steamer into the Pot, then close and lock the lid into place.
4. Set the manual timer to cook at high pressure for 1 minute. When the timer buzzes, release the steam manually.
5. Take the cauliflower out and pour the water out of the pot.
6. Turn the Instant Pot on sauté or warm setting.

7. Add the oil of your choice to the Instant Pot and then add the cooked cauliflower. Break it up with a potato masher.

8. While the cauliflower is heating up, add the spices you want. Continue stirring. Once the flavors have had time to seep together, remove the cauliflower. Add lime juice if desired and enjoy.

# *Sri Lankan Coconut Cabbage*

Per Serving – Fat: 8.2g/ Protein: 2.2g/ Carbs: 10.5g

## Ingredients:

- 1 Tbsp. coconut oil
- 1 medium onion (halved/sliced)
- 1 ½ tsp. salt
- 2 cloves garlic (diced)
- ½ long red chili pepper (sliced)
- 1 Tbsp. yellow mustard seeds (or 1 tsp. mustard powder)
- 1 Tbsp. curry powder
- 1 Tbsp. turmeric powder
- 1 medium cabbage (quartered and shredded with core removed)
- 1 carrot (peeled and sliced)
- 2 Tbsp. lime juice (can use lemon)
- ½ desiccated unsweetened coconut
- 1 Tbsp. olive or avocado oil
- 1/3 cup water

## Instructions:

1. Press the sauté button on the Instant Pot and put the coconut oil onion and a little of the salt in the pot. Let it sauté for three to four minutes until the onion is softened.
2. Add the garlic, chili pepper and spices and stir for about 30 seconds. Then add the cabbage, carrots, lime juice, coconut and olive oil. Stir. Then, add the water and stir again. Press the warm button.
3. Put the lid on and lock in place. Make sure the seal is set to close. Press the up arrow to set the Pot to cook at high pressure for five minutes. After it has beeped that it is finished, let the pressure release naturally for five minutes, then let off the rest of the steam using the manual quick release.

# *Pressure Steamed Artichoke*

Per Serving – Fat: 0g/ Protein: 2g/ Carbs: 6.8g

## Ingredients:

- Whole artichokes (whatever you can fit in a single layer in the IP)
- Lemon wedge
- Cup of water

## Instructions:

1. Rinse the artichokes with water and remove any outer leaves that may be damaged. Trim the stem and about 1/3 off the top. Rub the top with the lemon wedge. This prevents browning.
2. Set the steamer basket or steam rack in the Instant Pot and place the artichokes on top. Pour in the cup of water. Close and seal the lid.
3. Select "manual" and set the IP to cook on high pressure to cook for 5 minutes for a small artichoke, 10 for a medium-sized one and 15 for larger sizes.
4. When the cooking time is over, let it release steam naturally for 10 minutes, then release the remaining steam manually.
5. Remove the artichokes and serve with your favorite dipping sauce.

# *Creamy Cauliflower Soup*

Per Serving – Fat: 8.3g/ Protein: 6.4g/ Carbs: 7.5g

## Ingredients:

- 2 Tbsp. coconut oil
- ½ yellow onion sliced thinly
- 4 cloves of garlic sliced thinly
- 1 head of cauliflower – cut into florets
- 32 oz. vegetable broth
- 1 sprig fresh rosemary
- 2 tsp. sea salt (divided in half)
- ¾ tsp. chives
- 1 tsp. onion powder
- ½ tsp. smoked paprika

## Instructions:

1. Sauté the garlic cloves, coconut oil and onion in the Instant Pot for about a minute.
2. Add the fresh rosemary, half the salt, the cauliflower florets and the veggie broth to the Instant Pot. Close the lid and seal it. Cook on high pressure for 5 minutes. Let the steam release with the quick release method.
3. Remove the sprig of rosemary. Add the rest of the spices and stir.
4. Transfer the soup to the blender or use an immersion blender to blend until smooth. This should only take about 30 seconds or so.
5. Pour into bowls garnish with dried chives and enjoy!

# *Vegan Cream of Asparagus Soup*

Per Serving – Fat: 19.3g/ Protein: 8.7g/ Carbs: 4.8g

## Ingredients:

- About 1 lb. of asparagus spears
- Small onion chopped finely
- 2 Tbsp. avocado or olive oil
- 1 clove of garlic chopped finely
- 4 cups of vegetable broth
- ¾ cup coconut cream
- Salt and pepper to taste preference
- Olive oil for serving

## Instructions:

1. Trim the tough ends off and remove stem sections using a vegetable peeler if desired. Chop spears into one-inch pieces. Prepare onion and garlic.
2. Put the oil of your choice in the Instant Pot and press the sauté button. Add the onions and garlic and cook for a few minutes until the onion is soft.
3. Press the "keep warm" button and add the broth. Use a spoon to scrape any caramelized onions from the bottom. Add asparagus the place the lid on the pot and seal it.
4. Press the "manual" button and set to cook for 5 minutes. Then press start. When it is done, let the steam release naturally for 5 more minutes. Then, release the remaining steam carefully.
5. Use an immersion blender to cream the soup and make it smooth.
6. Add the coconut cream and salt and pepper to taste and stir to mix thoroughly.
7. Enjoy!

# Instant Pot Ketogenic Vegetarian Recipes

## *Soy Curl Butter "Chicken"*

Per Serving – Fat: 24g/ Protein: 5g/ Carbs: 6g

### Ingredients:

- 1 can diced tomatoes (14.5 oz.)
- 5 to 6 cloves of garlic
- 1 to 2 tsp. minced ginger
- 1 tsp. turmeric
- ½ tsp. cayenne pepper
- 1 tsp. paprika
- 1 tsp. salt (to taste)
- 1 tsp. garam masala
- 1 tsp. cumin
- 1.5 cups dry soy curls (may use firm tofu)
- 1 cup of water
- 4 oz. butter or coconut oil
- 4 oz. cream
- 1 tsp. garam masala
- ¼ to ½ cup fresh cilantro chopped

### Instructions:

1. Place the tomatoes, soy curls, water and spices into the Instant Pot and set it to cook on high pressure for 6 minutes. Let the pressure release naturally for 10 minutes, then release the rest of the pressure manually.
2. Turn on the sauté' feature and add the butter and cream. Continue to stir as they melt. Make sure to crush any large pieces of tomato that might be left.
3. Mix in the last teaspoon of garam masala and the cilantro.
4. Enjoy!

# *Mashed Cauliflower*

Per Serving – Fat: 11g/ Protein: 11g/ Carbs: 7g

## Ingredients:

- 2 small cauliflower crowns (or 1 large)
- 2 cups vegetable broth
- 2 Tbsp. butter
- ½ tsp. salt
- ½ tsp. garlic powder
- ¾ cup parmesan Reggiano cheese

## Instructions:

1. Place the trivet or steamer basket in the IP. Place the cauliflower and veggie broth in the pot.
2. Close the lid and seal it. Cook for three minutes on high pressure.
3. Use the quick release function.
4. Put the cauliflower in a food processor and add the butter, salt, garlic powder and parmesan cheese. Process it until it is silky smooth.
5. Serve immediately. Top with more butter if desired.

# *Zucchini and Yellow Squash Soup*

Per Serving – Fat: 25g/ Protein: 13.5g/ Carbs: 23g

## Ingredients:

- 2 Tbsp. olive oil or avocado oil
- 1 Tbsp. butter
- 1 yellow onion – chopped
- 1 Tbsp. fresh minced garlic
- 1 tsp. Italian herb blend
- 4 tsp. fresh chopped rosemary
- 3 lbs. of green and yellow summer squash
- 6 cups vegetable broth
- Salt and pepper to taste
- Fresh Parmesan for garnish

## Instructions:

1. Prepare all the veggies before you get started. Then heat the oil and butter in the Instant Pot using the sauté feature. Add the onion and sauté for about five minutes or until the onion is softened. Then add garlic, rosemary and the Italian herb blend. Cook for about five more minutes.

2. Add the vegetable broth to the mixture and simmer for about 10 minutes or until it is warm. Then add the squash mixture. Close, lock and seal the lid then cook for five minutes on high pressure setting. As soon as it is done, use the quick release method.

3. Puree the mixture with an immersion blender or using a food processor. Simmer the soup about 20 minutes using the sauté feature. Then season with salt and pepper.

4. Serve with topped with grated Parmesan cheese.

# *Garlic Ginger Red Cabbage*

Per Serving – Fat: 6.6g/ Protein: 1.4g/ Carbs: 6.3g

## Ingredients:

- 2 Tbsp. coconut oil
- 1 Tbsp. butter
- 3 cloves of garlic (crushed)
- 2 tsp. fresh ginger (grated)
- 8 cups of red cabbage (shredded)
- 1 tsp. salt
- ½ tsp. pepper
- 1/3 cup of water

## Instructions:

1. Press the sauté button, then add the butter and coconut oil. Once they are melted, then add the garlic and ginger. Mix well.
2. Add cabbage, salt, pepper and water.
3. Close the lid, seal and lock the vent.
4. Using the manual button, set it to cook on high pressure for 5 minutes.
5. Use the quick release method when it is done.
6. Mix well and serve.

# *Vegetarian Cream of Asparagus Soup*

Per Serving – Fat: 32.3g/ Protein: 8.7g/ Carbs: 4.8g (net)

## Ingredients:

- About 1 lb. of asparagus spears
- Small onion chopped finely
- 2 Tbsp. butter, ghee or avocado oil
- 1 clove of garlic chopped finely
- 4 cups of chicken stock or chicken bone broth
- ¾ cup heavy cream or coconut cream
- Salt and pepper to taste preference
- Olive oil for serving

## Instructions:

1. Trim the tough ends off and remove stem sections using a vegetable peeler if desired. Chop spears into one-inch pieces. Prepare onion and garlic.
2. Put the ghee or butter in the Instant Pot and press the sauté button. Add the onions and garlic and cook for a few minutes until the onion is soft.
3. Press the "keep warm" button and add the chicken broth. Use a spoon to scrape any caramelized onions from the bottom. Add asparagus the place the lid on the pot and seal it.
4. Press the "manual" button and set to cook for 5 minutes. Then press start. When it is done, let the steam release naturally for 5 more minutes. Then, release the remaining steam carefully.
5. Use an immersion blender to cream the soup and make it smooth.
6. Add the coconut cream and salt and pepper to taste and stir to mix thoroughly.
7. Enjoy!

# *Cream of Celery Soup*

Per Serving – Fat: 14.6g/ Protein: 2.7g/ Carbs: 6g

## Ingredients:

- 1 large bunch of celery (should make about 6 cups)
- 1 sweet yellow onion
- 1 cup of coconut milk
- 2 cups of water (or veggie broth)
- ½ tsp. dill
- Pinch of salt

## Instructions:

1. Dice the celery and onion. Then, add all the ingredients to the Instant Pot.
2. Place the lid on the IP, seal it and then press the "soup" function.
3. This will automatically set the Instant Pot to cook for 30 minutes and shift into "keep warm" mode when done.
4. Once the Instant Pot has depressurized, take the lid off and blend the soup until it is creamy using an immersion blender. It can also be poured into a blender or food processor. Just remember it is hot so be careful.

# Instant Pot Ketogenic Main Course Recipes

## *Corned Beef and Cabbage Dinner*

Per Serving – Fat: 60g/ Protein: 60g/ Carbs: 9g

### Ingredients:

- 3.5 lbs. of corned beef brisket (with spices)
- Small head of cabbage
- 2 cups baby carrots
- 5 cups water

### Instructions:

1. Drain and rinse the corn beef if it is cured. Otherwise, it does not need to be drained. Place it in the Instant pot then add water – about 5 cups.
2. Close and lock the lid. Set the timer to high pressure for 90 minutes.
3. When it is done, quick release the steam. Check to see if the meet is done. If it is not, cook for another 10 minutes on high pressure.
4. Cut the cabbage into 8 wedges. Place the cabbage wedges and carrots in the IP with the corned beef being careful to not overfill the Instant Pot.
5. Replace the lid, set the timer to cook for 5 minutes at high pressure.
6. When the cycle has completed, use the quick release method to release the steam. Take out the veggies and beef. Slice the beef against the grain – and enjoy!

# Indian Kheema

Per Serving – Fat: 20g/ Protein: 29g/ Carbs: 6g

## Ingredients:

- 1 cup onions chopped finely
- 1 Tbsp. ghee, avocado oil or olive oil
- 1 Tbsp. minced ginger
- 1 Tbsp. garlic
- 3 to 4 cinnamon stick pieces
- 4 pods of green or white cardmo
- 1 lb. of ground beef
- 1 Tbsp. garam masala
- 1 Tbsp. salt
- ½ tsp. turmeric
- ½ tsp. cayenne pepper (adjust to personal heat level)
- ½ tsp. ground coriander
- ½ tsp. cumin
- ¼ cup of water

## Instructions:

1. Turn on the sauté button on your Instant Pot. Add oil of your choice and let it warm. Then add the cinnamon sticks and cardamom. Let sizzle for about 10 seconds. Then add the onions, garlic and ginger. Let it cook for 3 to 5 minutes.
2. Add the ground beef. Sauté just long enough to break up the clumps, about 3 to 4 minutes.
3. Add spices and water. Close and seal the Instant Pot.
4. Cook for 5 minutes on high pressure. Allow the pressure to release naturally for 10 minutes, then manually release the rest of the pressure.
5. Serve and enjoy!

# *Italian Pulled Pork Ragu*

Per Serving – Fat: 1.5g/ Protein: 11g/ Carbs: 6.5g

## Ingredients:

- 18 oz. of pork tenderloin
- 1 tsp. salt
- Ground black pepper to taste
- 1 tsp. olive oil or avocado oil
- 5 garlic cloves (mashed)
- 1 can of crushed tomatoes (28 oz. can)
- 1 (7 oz.) jar roasted red peppers (drained)
- 2 sprigs thyme
- 2 bay leaves
- 1 Tbsp. chopped fresh parsley

## Instructions:

1. Season the pork with salt and pepper. Then turn on the sauté button on the Instant Pot. Warm the oil and sauté the garlic for a minute or two until it is brown. Remove the garlic, leaving the oil.
2. Add pork and brown it for about 2 minutes on each side, then add the rest of the ingredients except for half the fresh parsley. Also, add the garlic back into the mix.
3. Cook using the high pressure setting for 45 minutes.
4. Let it release the pressure naturally.
5. Remove the bay leaves and discard. Then shred the pork with two forks. And top with the remaining half of the parsley.
6. Serve over zoodles or cauliflower-rice.

# *Ground Beef Shawarma*

Per Serving – Fat: 7g/ Protein: 25g/ Carbs: 8g

## Ingredients:

- 1 lb. of ground beef
- 1 cup sliced onions
- 1 cup thickly sliced red peppers
- 2 cups of cabbage chopped into chunks
- 2 Tbsp. shawarma mix (recipe below)
- 1 tsp. salt

*Shawarma Mix Recipe:*

- 2 tsp. dried oregano
- 1 tsp. ground cinnamon
- ½ tsp. ground allspice
- ½ tsp. cayenne pepper
- 1 tsp. cumin
- 1 tsp. coriander
- 1 to 2 tsp. salt

Grind the spices together in coffee grinder.

## Instructions:

1. Turn the sauté button on. Then add the beef and let it cook while you use a spoon to break it down so there are no big chunks.
2. After the meat is browned, add all the other ingredients. You won't need water as the meat will cook down and provide enough moisture.
3. Set the Pot to cook on high pressure for 2 minutes. Then, let it release the pressure naturally for five minutes before manually releasing the rest.
4. May be served with a side of tzatziki sauce to increase the fat content of the meal.

# *Creamy Salsa Chicken*

Per Serving – Fat: 12g/ Protein: 43g/ Carbs: 4g

## Ingredients:

- Chicken breasts (2 ½ to 3 lbs.)
- ½ cup chicken broth
- 4 oz. cream cheese
- ½ cup cottage cheese
- 1 cup salsa (check ingredients or make your own)
- 1 tsp. taco seasoning (can be made yourself)
- Optional toppings include: shredded cheese, sour cream, avocado, chopped tomatoes

*Taco Seasoning:*

- 1 Tbsp. chili powder
- ¼ tsp. garlic powder
- ¼ tsp. onion powder
- ¼ tsp. crushed red pepper flakes (optional)
- ½ tsp. paprika
- 1/4 tsp. oregano
- 1 ½ tsp. cumin
- 1 tsp. salt (optional)

## Instructions:

1. Place the chicken breasts and broth in the Instant Pot. Close and seal the Pot then use the poultry setting to cook for 10 minutes.
2. Quick release the pressure and use a meat thermometer to ensure it is at least 160 degrees. Remove the chicken to a bowl and save ½ cup of the stock.

3. Add the ½ cup of stock and all the other ingredients. Then whisk until the cheeses are melted. Turn the "keep warm" feature on.
4. Shred the chicken and add it back to the sauce and mix.
5. Serve with any combination of the optional toppings.

# *Green Chili Pork Taco Bowl*

Per Serving – Fat: 23.9g/ Protein: 64g/ Carbs: 6.6g

## Ingredients:

- 2 lbs. of pork sirloin roast
- 2 tsp. cumin
- 2 tsp. garlic powder
- 1 tsp. salt
- 1 tsp. ground black pepper
- 1 Tbsp. olive oil
- 16 oz. green chili tomatillo salsa (choose a sugar free brand)

*For Serving:*

- Large poblano chili pepper
- Limes
- Grated cheese blend
- Sour cream
- Avocado slices

## Instructions:

1. Trim the roast into thick slices. Cut against the grain so when it is shredded later you can get shorter pieces.
2. Mix the cumin, garlic powder and salt and pepper together then rub both sides of the meat with it.
3. Put some oil in the Instant Pot and turn on the sauté function. Once the oil is hot, cook the meat until it is browned on both sides. Pour the tomatillo sauce on top of the meat. Cook at high pressure for 45 minutes.
4. When it is done, use natural release for 20 minutes. Then release any remaining pressure manually. Take the pork out of the pot and shred it.
5. Serve over a bed of lettuce, or cauliflower rice if desired. Use your favorite taco toppings.

# *No Noodle Lasagna*

Per Serving – Fat: 25g/ Protein: 25g/ Carbs: 7g

## Ingredients:

- 1 lb. of ground beef
- 2 garlic cloves minced
- 1 small onion
- 1 ½ cups ricotta cheese
- ½ cup parmesan cheese
- 1 large egg
- 1 jar marinara sauce (no sugar brand – or make your own)
- 8 oz. sliced mozzarella

## Instructions:

1. Use the sauté setting to brown the meet along with the onion and the garlic.
2. While the meat is browning, combine the egg, ricotta cheese and parmesan cheese in a small bowl.
3. Remove the browned beef to a soufflé dish, or other dish that fits in the Instant Pot. Add marinara sauce to the meat. Divide in half and top the bowl of meat sauce with half the mozzarella cheese. Then spread the ricotta cheese mixture on top.
4. Place the rest of the meat sauce on top and add mozzarella cheese and ricotta again.
5. Wrap the dish with aluminum foil so it will not leak into the IP.
6. Pour 1 cup of water in the Instant Pot and put the soufflé dish on a rack inside. Pressure on high for 8 to 10 minutes. When it is done, let the steam out manually.
7. Dip into bowls for serving and sprinkle with parmesan cheese.
8. Enjoy!

# *Creamy Chicken and Broccoli Casserole*

Per Serving – Fat: 31.8g/ Protein: 13.4g/ Carbs: 6g

## Ingredients:

- 2 heads broccoli
- 3 chicken breasts
- 1 cup keto mayo
- 2/3 cup heavy cream
- 1 Tbsp. chicken soup base
- 1 Tbsp. dried dill weed
- 1 tsp. black pepper
- 2 cups shredded cheddar cheese
- ½ cup chicken or veggie broth

## Instructions:

1. Place the chicken breasts and broth in the Instant Pot. Cook on high pressure for 8 minutes. Quick release the rest of the pressure when it is done. Remove chicken and shred with two forks.
2. Press the sauté button and add broccoli. Let it cook for about 3 minutes, or until it starts to soften.
3. Then add mayo, cream, soup base, dill week and the chicken. Stir thoroughly. Remove from Instant Pot and add shredded cheese. Stir and let the cheese melt throughout the mixture.

# Sausage, Zucchini and Cauliflower Risotto

Per Serving – Fat: 37.8g/ Protein: 14.9g/ Carbs: 12.1g

## Ingredients:

- ¼ cup ghee
- ½ onion chopped finely
- 1 clove of garlic minced
- 2 links of chicken sausage cut into ½-inch rounds
- 1 head of cauliflower – grated
- ½ zucchini sliced
- ½ cup heavy cream
- 1 cup grated Parmesan cheese
- ½ tsp. salt
- ¼ tsp. pepper
- ¼ tsp. nutmeg

## Instructions:

1. Press the sauté button on the Instant Pot. Add ghee and let melt. Then add the onion and garlic cooking them until they are tender. Just about 3 minutes. Stir in the grated cauliflower and sausage and cook about 3 minutes, then add the zucchini and cook about 3 more minutes until it is tender.
2. Stir in the heavy cream, Parmesan cheese, salt, pepper and nutmeg. Then put the lid on and close it. Press the manual button and set to cook on high pressure for 3 minutes. Quick release the pressure.
3. Enjoy!

# *Stuffed Pepper Casserole*

Per Serving – Fat: 16.5g/ Protein: 19.2g/ Carbs: 9.8g

## Ingredients:

- 1 head of cauliflower, broken into small florets
- 1 lb. of ground beef
- ½ cup onion chopped
- 2 cloves of garlic minced
- 3 green bell peppers chopped
- Italian seasoning or to taste
- 1 can diced tomatoes drained
- ¾ cup beef broth
- 2 cups shredded cheddar cheese

## Instructions:

1. Put cauliflower florets into a food processor and pulse into "rice." Set aside.
2. Press the sauté button on the Instant Pot and combine meat, onion and garlic. Cook and continue to stir until the meat is brown and the onion is tender. Add the bell peppers and Italian seasoning. Cook until the peppers are tender, just about 2 minutes.
3. Drain any excess oil from the meat mixture. Add tomatoes and beef broth. Leave on sauté for about 5 minutes and let it simmer. Add the cauliflower.
4. Press the manual button on the IP and set it to cook on high power for 5 minutes. Allow the steam to release naturally for 2 minutes, then do a quick release.
5. Stir in the cheddar cheese and brown in oven if desired.

# *Pork Chops with Cabbage*

Per Serving – Fat: 14.7g/ Protein: 25.1g/ Carbs: 8.4g

## Ingredients:

- 4 thick-cut pork chops
- 1 tsp. fennel seeds
- 1 tsp. salt
- 1 tsp. pepper
- 1 small head of cabbage
- 1 Tbsp. olive or avocado oil
- ¾ cup meat broth

## Instructions:

1. Sprinkle the pork chops with salt, pepper and fennel.
2. Prepare the cabbage by slicing it into ¾-inch slices and then set it aside.
3. Press the sauté button on the Instant Pot. Add the oil. Once it's hot brown the pork chops on one side only. Then set them aside.
4. Add the cabbage slices to the Instant Pot. Place the pork chops (brown side up) on top of the cabbage. Pour any juice left from the pork chops and the meat broth around the edges. Cover with the lid and lock in place.
5. Cook on high pressure for 8 minutes. When the cooker is done, use quick release to allow the pressure to escape.
6. Place the pork chops on the cabbage and pour a little bit of the juice on top of them.
7. Serve and enjoy!

# *Pork and Kraut*

Per Serving – Fat: 19g/ Protein: 44.6g/ Carbs: 9.2g

## Ingredients:

- 2 to 3 lbs. pork roast
- 2 Tbsp. coconut oil, ghee, butter (your choice of oil)
- 2 large onions (slice or chop)
- 3 cloves garlic (sliced)
- 1 cup water
- Sea salt and pepper to taste
- 4-6 cups sauerkraut

## Instructions:

1. Salt and pepper the roast. Press the sauté button on the Instant Pot. Add your choice of oil and then brown the pork roast on all sides.
2. Turn off the Instant Pot and clean inside container before proceeding.
3. Place the rack in the IP. Add water, garlic, and onions. Add salt and pepper if desired.
4. Press the manual button to set the roast to cook for 35 minutes under high pressure. When it is done, let the pressure release naturally. After the Instant Pot has depressurized, add in the sauerkraut. You may add in only half and save the other half to eat uncooked for the health benefits.
5. Replace the lid and seal in place. Cook 5 minutes on high pressure setting. If the roast needs to cook longer, you can cook up to 15 minutes on high pressure.
6. Use a quick release to depressurize.

# *Hungarian Goulash*

Per Serving – Fat: 23.9g/ Protein: 23.8g/ Carbs: 8.33g

## Ingredients:

- 2 Tbsp. bacon grease, olive oil, lard, butter or avocado oil
- 1 cup chopped onions
- 2 Tbsp. Hungarian paprika (not Spanish/smoked)
- 2 cloves of garlic
- 2 lbs. of beef stew meat cubed
- 1 tsp. salt
- ½ tsp. pepper
- ½ tsp. caraway seeds
- 2 cups cubed daikon radish
- 1 chopped pepper – yellow or green
- 2 sliced celery stalks
- 1 (15 oz.) can of diced tomatoes
- 1 ½ cups chicken, beef or vegetable broth
- 1 bay leaf

## Instructions:

1. Put the oil of your choice in the Instant Pot and press sauté. When the oil is hot, add the meat and brown it on all sides. Once it is browned, remove it from the IP, and set it aside. Add the onion, caraway seeds and bell pepper to the oil and cook for 5 minutes. Then add the garlic and sauté until it is fragrant.

2. Add radish pepper, celery, tomatoes, broth and the bay leaf. Add the meat back in as well.

3. Press the sauté button to turn it off. Then place the lid on the pot and seal it.

4. Push the stew button and set it to cook for 25 minutes. When it is done, allow the steam to release naturally for 10 minutes, then manually release the rest of the pressure.

5. Serve it as a soup or over zoodles. You can also add sour cream if desired.

# *Pulled Pork Carnitas*

Per Serving – Fat: 25g/ Protein: 65g/ Carbs: 3g

## Ingredients:

- 4 lbs. of pork roast (leg or shoulder are best)
- 2 Tbsp. olive or avocado oil
- 1 head of butter lettuce
- 2 spiralized or grated carrots (optional)
- 2 limes cut into wedges

*Spice Mix Ingredients:*

- 1 Tbsp. unsweetened cocoa powder
- 1 Tbsp. salt
- 1 tsp. red pepper flakes
- 2 tsp. oregano
- 1 tsp. white pepper
- 1 tsp. garlic powder
- 1 tsp. cumin
- ½ tsp. coriander
- 1/8 tsp. cayenne pepper
- 1 large onion chopped finely

## Instructions:

1. The day before you plan to cook the meat, mix the spices together. Cut the roast into smaller pieces and then rub them with the spice mix. Wrap it all back up and place it in the fridge overnight.

2. Set the Instant Pot to sauté and add a little oil. Cook until it is brown on all sides. Add enough water to almost cover the meat. That should be about 2 to 3 cups. Close the led and seal. Cook the meat for 50 minutes on high pressure.

3. When it is done, let the steam release naturally on its own. Once it has released all the steam, take the meat out and put it on a plate or platter. Use a couple of forks to shred the meat.

4. Pour out the liquid left in the Instant Pot. You may want to de-fat it and use it for other recipes.

5. You can refrigerate the meat at this point if you want it ready for a get together later.

6. When you are ready to serve the meat or meal, turn the IP on sauté. Add the olive oil and heat the shredded pork up until it is slightly browned.

7. Make lettuce wraps by preparing lettuce "cups.". Fill them with the fried pork and top with the shredded carrots. Squirt with fresh lime juice. You can also leave the carrots off to cut some carbs.

# *Boeuf Bourguignon with Veggies*

Per Serving – Fat: 32g/ Protein: 50g/ Carbs: 6g

## Ingredients:

- 5 slices of thick cut bacon, cubed
- 3 lbs. of beef chuck roast, cut into 1-inch cubes
- Salt and pepper
- Large yellow onion
- 3 whole celery stalks, diced
- 3 minced cloves of garlic
- 1 Tbsp. tomato paste
- 1 lb. of small white button mushrooms
- 4 sprigs fresh thyme
- 1 bay leaf
- 1 cup of chicken or beef broth (may need a little more than one cup)
- 1 cup of red wine
- 1 large carrot (or two medium carrots spiralized)
- Parsley for garnish
- If you like heat – use red pepper flakes for garnish

## Instructions:

1. Using the sauté setting on the Instant Pot, cook the bacon until it is crispy. Once it is done, remove it and place the strips on a paper towel.
2. Season the cubed beef roast with salt and pepper.
3. Add the beef cubes to the Instant pot and sear for 1 to 3 minutes, until they are seared on all sides. Add the cooked bacon, onion, celery, garlic and mushrooms to the Instant Pot with the meat. Place the bay leaf and thyme in with the vegetables.

Pour the broth and wine over the meats and vegetables. They should be about ¾ covered with liquid.

4. Place the lid on the Instant Pot, close it and seal it. Use the slow cooker function and cook on high for four hours. At the end of four hours, remove the lid and add the carrots. Cook for one more hour in the slow cooker.

5. When it is done, remove the bay leaves. Stir it all up and serve it in bowls. Garnish with red pepper flakes and parsley.

# Instant Pot Ketogenic Side Dish Recipes

## *Cauliflower Rice and Cheese*

Per 1-cup Serving – Fat: 13g/ Protein: 7g/ Carbs: 5g

## Ingredients:

- 1 Head of riced cauliflower
- 75 grams chopped or shredded cheese
- 2 oz. cream cheese
- ¼ tsp. garlic powder
- 4 slices cooked and chopped bacon
- ¼ tsp. salt (to taste, or optional)

## *Instructions:*

1. Mix all the ingredients together in a heat-proof bowl.
2. Use aluminum foil to cover the bowl.
3. Put one and a half cups of water in the bottom of the Instant Pot. Then put in the trivet and place the covered bowl on top of it.
4. Set the Instant Pot to cook on high pressure for 5 minutes. When it is done, allow it to release naturally for at least 10 minutes.
5. Place the cooked dish in the oven under the broiler to brown the cheese if desired.
6. Enjoy!

# *Spaghetti Squash with Sage-Garlic Sauce*

Per serving (makes 4) – Fat: 4g/ Protein: 1.5g/ Carbs: 7g

## Ingredients:

- Small to medium spaghetti squash
- 1 cup water
- Small bunch of fresh sage (you need about ½ cup of fresh sage leaves)
- 3 sliced garlic cloves
- 2 Tbsp. olive oil (avocado oil or coconut oil)
- 1 tsp. salt
- 1/8 tsp. grated nutmeg

## Instructions:

1. Spaghetti squash should be cut in half and the seeds removed by scooping them out.
2. Add one cup of water to the IP, place the two halves in the pot facing upward. You can stack them on top of one another.
3. Close the lid, lock into place and close the steam valve. Cook the squash on high pressure for 6 minutes.
4. After it is done, release the pressure, and remove the squash when it has cooled.
5. In another pan, sauté the sage, garlic and olive oil.
6. Remove the squash fibers from the shell and put it in the pan with the spices. Sprinkle with salt and nutmeg, then mix well.
7. Serve as is. Or just add a bit of cheese.

# *Zoodles with Lemon, Garlic and Parmesan*

Per Serving – Fat: 1.6g/ Protein: 3.4 g/ Carbs: 4g

## Ingredients:

- 2 Tbsp. olive oil or avocado oil
- 2 cloves of garlic, dived
- Zest of half a lemon
- ½ tsp. salt
- 2 large zucchinis, spiralized (or peeled into noodle-ribbons)
- Juice of 1/3 lemon
- 1 Tbsp. mint – about 5 to 6 leaves (finely sliced)
- 4 Tbsp. grated Pecorino or Parmesan cheese
- Black pepper

## Instructions:

1. Prepare all the ingredients before starting to cook.
2. After all the ingredients are gathered and ready, turn on the sauté feature on the Instant Pot. Let it heat for just a minute or two, then add the oil, garlic, lemon zest and salt if desired. Stir it until it is brown and fragrant, about 30 seconds is all.
3. Add the zucchini noodles. Drizzle the lemon juice over them. Stir it all up for another 20 to 30 seconds, just enough to coat the noodles. They should get warm, but not actually cook.
4. After the noodles are warm, sprinkle with mint and cheese of your choice then serve immediately.

# *Bacon Parmesan Spaghetti Squash*

Per Serving – Fat: 7g/ Protein: 6g/ Carbs: 5.3g

## Ingredients:

- 4 slices bacon
- 1 medium sized spaghetti squash
- A pinch of salt
- 1 ½ Tbsp. olive oil or avocado oil
- ½ cup course-grated Parmigiano Reggiano
- Pepper to taste

## Instructions:

1. To prepare the spaghetti squash, poke some holes in the squash with a knife. Then put it in the Instant Pot. Set it to cook on high pressure for 12 minutes. Release the steam once it's done and then cut the squash in half and remove the seeds. Then remove the squash "noodles."
2. While the squash is cooking in the Instant Pot, fry the bacon and then cut it into pieces.
3. Mix the spaghetti squash noodles with the bacon, oil and Parmesan.

# *Brussels Sprouts with Bacon*

Per Serving – Fat: 8g/ Protein: 6g/ Carbs: 5g

## Ingredients:

- 2 lbs. of halved Brussels sprouts
- ¼ cup soy sauce
- 2 Tbsp. sriracha sauce
- 1 Tbsp. rice vinegar
- 2 Tbsp. sesame, avocado or olive oil
- 4 strips of thick bacon
- 1 Tbsp. almonds
- 1 tsp. red pepper flakes
- 2 tsp. garlic powder
- 1 tsp. onion powder
- 1 Tbsp. smoked paprika
- ½ tsp. cayenne pepper (more if you like it hot!)
- Salt and pepper as desired

## Instructions:

1. Put the cooked, chopped bacon and chopped almonds in the Instant Pot on sauté mode. Sauté for just a couple minutes, until warm.
2. Mix in all the seasonings and liquids.
3. Add the Brussels sprouts.
4. Cook on high pressure for 2 minutes and do a quick release when they are done. If they are cooked too long, they get too soft and mushy.
5. Enjoy as a stand-alone side dish or eat over cauliflower rice.

# *Asparagus Wrapped in Prosciutto*

Serving – Fat: 3.3g/ Protein: 14.4g/ Carbs: 5.3g

## Ingredients:

- 1 lb. of Asparagus (thick asparagus works best)
- 8 oz. of thinly sliced prosciutto

## Instructions:

1. Put the minimum amount of water in your Instant Pot. This may be one or two cups depending on what the instruction booklet recommends.
2. Wrap the prosciutto around the asparagus spears. Put any leftover unwrapped spears in a steamer basket. Then place the wrapped spears layered on top. This keeps the prosciutto from sticking to the bottom of the basket.
3. Place the basket in the IP. Close and seal the lid. Use the manual button and set the IP to cook on high pressure for 2 to 3 minutes. As soon as the spears are done, release the steam from the IP manually.
4. Remove the steamer basket and serve asparagus on a platter.

# *Ham and Greens*

Per Serving – Fat: 6.5g/ Protein: 4g/ Carbs: 9g

## Ingredients:

- 6 to 8 cups collard greens
- 1 large chopped onion
- 6 garlic cloves
- 2 cups chopped, cooked ham
- 1 tsp. salt
- 1 tsp. pepper
- ¼ cup water or veggie stock
- 1 tsp. red pepper flakes
- 2 bay leaves
- 1 tsp. dried thyme

*Optional for Finishing:*

- 1 Tbsp. apple cider vinegar
- 1 tsp. vinegar based hot sauce
- 1 tsp. liquid smoke

## Instructions:

1. Place all the ingredients in the Instant Pot, except for the optional finishing ingredients.
2. Set the IP to cook at high pressure for 4 minutes. After it has finished, allow it to release naturally for 5 minutes and then slowly release the remaining pressure.
3. Add the optional finishing ingredients as desired.
4. Enjoy.

# *Carrot Pasta*

Per Serving – Fat: 15.7g/ Protein: 9.3g/ Carbs: 11.2g

## Ingredients:

- 6-8 carrots
- 4 slices bacon
- Large onion
- 5 tomatoes
- 2 Tbsp. coconut oil
- 2 Tbsp. thyme
- 1 Tbsp. parsley
- 1 Tbsp. powdered mustard
- Salt and pepper to taste

## Instructions:

1. Place a cup of water in the bottom of the Instant Pot and place the steamer basket inside.
2. Peel the carrots with a julienne peeler or use a spiralizer so they are more like noodles. Sprinkle them with salt, pepper, thyme and mustard powder. Toss the carrots so they are well covered with spices.
3. Put them in the steamer basket and place the lid on the IP and seal it. Set the steam function to cook for 15 minutes. As soon as it is done, manually release the remaining pressure. Remove the basket and water from the Instant Pot.
4. Turn the IP on sauté and add the coconut oil, chopped up bacon, chopped onion and remaining seasonings. Sauté for 5 minutes, or until the onion is crispy and the bacon is cooked.
5. Stir the bacon and onion mixture into the carrots and top with fresh quartered tomatoes.

# *Spinach and Artichoke Dip (Like Applebee's!)*

Per Serving – Fat: 26g/ Protein: 15g/ Carbs: 6g

## Ingredients:

- 8 oz. cream cheese
- 10 oz. box frozen spinach
- 16 oz. of shredded parmesan cheese
- 8 oz. of mozzarella cheese
- ½ cup chicken broth
- 14 oz. can of artichoke hearts
- ½ cup sour cream
- ½ cup (no-sugar) mayo
- 3 cloves of garlic
- 1 tsp. onion powder

## Instructions:

1. Place the ½ cup of chicken broth and the 3 cloves of garlic in the Instant Pot. Drain the artichokes and place them in the IP. Add the rest of the ingredients to the Instant Pot.
2. Cook on high pressure for 4 minutes. Do a quick release when the cycle is done.

# *Creamed Cauliflower and Spinach*

Per Serving – Fat: 6.4g/ Protein: 5.8g/ Carbs: 7.1g

## Ingredients:

- 5 oz. baby spinach
- Small head of cauliflower
- ½ cup shredded mozzarella cheese
- 2 Tbsp. cream
- 1 Tbsp. butter
- ½ tsp. nutmeg
- Pinch of cloves
- Salt and pepper to taste

## Instructions:

1. Put a cup of water in the Instant Pot and the steamer. Place the cauliflower in the IP and steam for 3 minutes. Remove and put through food processor with the cream and butter. Salt and pepper to taste.
2. Use the sauté function on the Instant Pot and sauté the onion in a little butter until soft. Then add the spinach, nutmeg and cloves. Continue to sauté until the spinach is wilted.
3. Mix the sautéed vegetables with the cauliflower. Top with a little mozzarella cheese. Put it in a dish under the broiler to brown the top of the cheese.

# Conclusion

Cooking with the Instant Pot is more than just the latest craze. It is fun, yes, but there are many benefits as well, including reduced cooking time. Maybe you thought you couldn't use the IP when on a specific eating plan like the ketogenic diet. Actually, there is so much you can do to help you on your keto diet adventure. There are tons of things that can be prepared using the Instant Pot.

### *What about meal prep?*

It has become common for family chefs to do a lot of meal prep. This can cut down on prep time during the busy weeks. By cooking up meals or large quantities of foods all at one time, and storing them properly, prep time is reduced greatly later. The Instant Pot lets you cook up meats or main courses that can be eaten over the following week. It will help you stay with the ketogenic eating plan if you have foods readily available. It will help reduce the urge to cheat or grab something fast whether it is the right choice or not. Meal prep is convenient and can help you stay on your eating plan. The IP can help reduce your cooking time, so you are in the kitchen less of the time and out with friends or family more.

We hope you enjoy preparing these carefully chosen ketogenic recipes. And we hope you have lots of fun trying a few creations of your own in your Instant Pot.

Made in the USA
Lexington, KY
22 July 2018